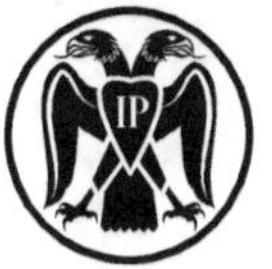

Imperium Press was founded in 2018 to supply students and laymen with works in the history of rightist thought. If these works are available at all in modern editions, they are rarely ever available in editions that place them where they belong: outside the liberal weltanschauung. Imperium Press' mission is to provide right thinkers with authoritative editions of the works that make up their own canon. These editions include introductions and commentary which place these canonical works squarely within the context of tradition, reaction, and counter-Enlightenment thought—the only context in which they can be properly understood.

# BLOOD,
# SOIL,
# PAINT

## ALEXANDER ADAMS

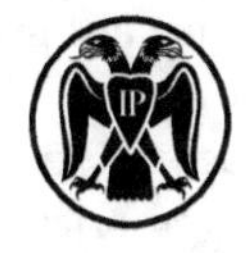

PERTH
IMPERIUM PRESS
2023

Published by Imperium Press
www.imperiumpress.org

© Alexander Adams, 2023
The moral rights of the author have been asserted
Used under license to Imperium Press

All rights are reserved. No part of this publication may be
reproduced, stored in a retrieval system, or transmitted in any
form or by any means, electronic, mechanical, photocopying,
recording, or otherwise, without prior permission of Imperium
Press. Enquiries concerning reproduction outside the scope of
the above should be directed to Imperium Press.

FIRST EDITION

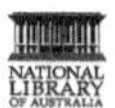

A catalogue record for this
book is available from the
National Library of Australia

ISBN 978-1-922602-73-2 Paperback
ISBN 978-1-922602-74-9 Hardcover
ISBN 978-1-922602-75-6 E-book

Imperium Press has no responsibility for the persistence or
accuracy of URLs for external or third-party Internet websites
referred to in this publication and does not guarantee that
any content on such websites is, or will remain, accurate or
appropriate.

# CONTENTS

BY THE SAME AUTHOR

Verse

*Three Strikes* (2011)
*The Crows of Berlin* (2013)
*On Dead Mountain* (2015)
*On Art* (2018)
*On Art II* (2020)
*After/Après Francis Bacon* (2022)

Fiction

*Letter About Spain* (2016)
*Berlin, October* (2016)
*London, Winter* (2017)
*Selima in the Orchard* (2018)

Art

*Works on Paper* (2004)
*Noctes* (2005)
*Icarus* (2005)
*Ruins and Landscapes* (2007)
*Paintings on Paper* (2008)
*New Gouaches* (2010)
*Portraiture* (2013)
*Nouvelles Peintures* (2018)

Non-Fiction

*Culture War: Art, Identity Politics & Cultural Entryism* (2019)
*Iconoclasm, Identity Politics and the Erasure of History* (2020)
*Artivism: The Battle for Museums in the Postmodern Era* (2022)
*Women and Art: A Post-Feminist View* (2022)
*Degas* (2022)
*Magritte* (2022)
*Dalí* (2023)

*For Amy,*

*with my love,*

*A.*

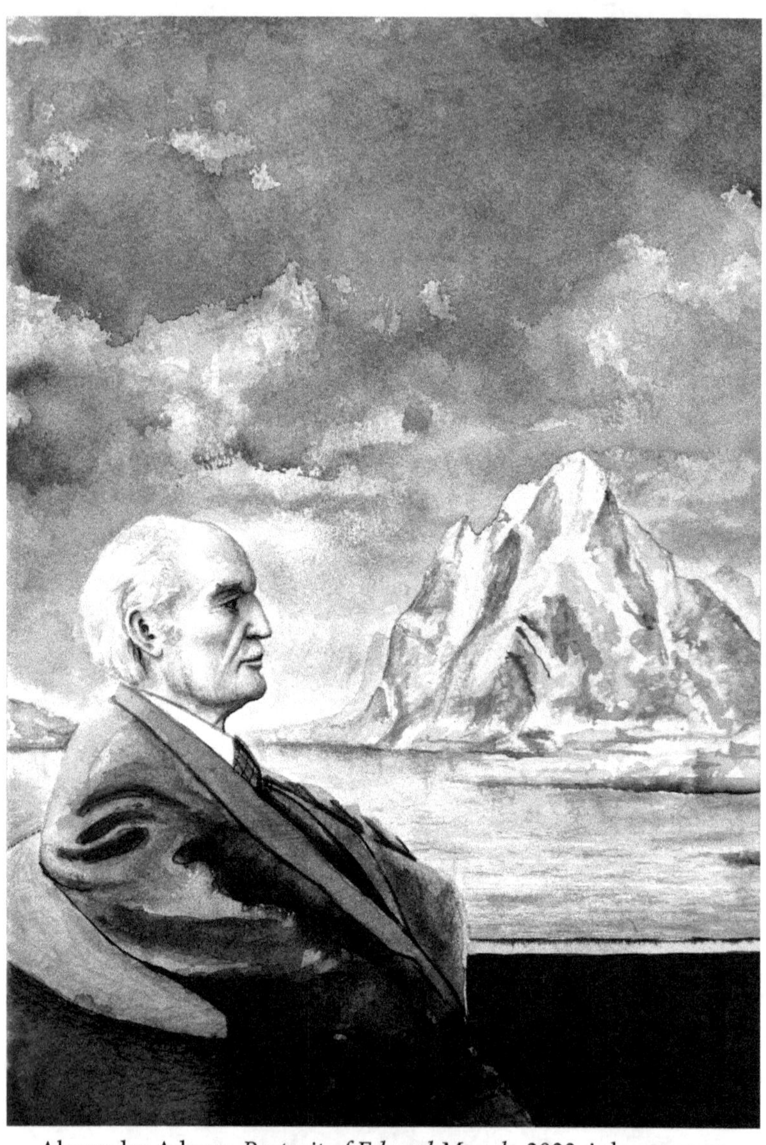

Alexander Adams, *Portrait of Edvard Munch,* 2022, ink on paper,
36 x 25 cm/14” x 10”

# BLOOD,
# SOIL,
# PAINT

# INTRODUCTION

---

The connections between Romanticism, nationalism, national character and the visual arts, especially in the context of Northern European countries, is a rich field. Too rich for a single book to cover. *Blood, Soil, Paint: An Essay on Romanticism, Nationalism and Art* is my initial contribution to the field. "Essay" has multiple meanings, one of them being "effort" or "test". *Blood, Soil, Paint* is by no means exhaustive or definitive, not even of my own thoughts, and is limited in scope. It is influenced by the years I have spent looking at, thinking about and discussing fine art, so this essay comes from the perspective of an artist and art critic. *Blood, Soil, Paint* discusses German and Russian Romantic artists, painters Edvard Munch and Anselm Kiefer, author Knut Hamsun and philosopher Martin Heidegger. One could nominate several dozen alternative creators of stature as similarly appropriate. The starting points were two exhibitions and catalogues that I reviewed in mid-2022, and a course on aesthetic philosophy that I wrote. As I thought more, ideas on national character, nationalism in Northern Europe and Romanticism generated a series of overlaps and recursive references that wound together as I wrote. It was only when the essay was reaching completion that I remembered a letter I had written in 2006,[1] which ends this essay, showing readers where my personal journey began.

When I commenced work on this essay, I did not have fixed views on the degree to which national character exerts influence in a man's daily thought and action, nor to what degree national character was genetic, environmental, or cultural in origin. Thinkers more significant and respected than me have believed that national character exists and is the destiny of men, whom they consider tied to each other through kinship (blood) and tied to the land (soil). What is indisputable is that since 1945, most public expressions of such sentiments have been guarded and qualified, tainted as they are by association with political movements considered by the liberalist consensus as irredeemable. Readers are invited to consult other books for historical and narrative approaches to the area; some of these are listed in the bibliography.

Whatever one's political inclination, one comes to recognise patterns and to discriminate on the basis of observations of individuals based on sex, age, ethnicity and nationality (as well as region). "Discrimination" here means informed judgement. This has been described as a shortcut—a "fast way of thinking"—and a route to making snap judgements based on visceral instincts, to be adjusted later when more detailed information comes to hand about specific subjects.[2] We find in the actions of people of all outlooks a strong reliance on instinct when the most crucial decisions must be reached. Unconscious bias and sub-verbal understanding are the foundation of our daily existence, however objective we consider ourselves to be, and no matter the fact that this intuition can sometimes be incomplete, inaccurate, misleading, and manipulable. Those who are convinced of the idea of national character, believe that such region-specific complexes of advantageous environmental and inter-personal knowledge have evolved to instantiate general truths that are vital and unchanging. How these values are shared between members of a group and passed down through generations—by observation, education, language, physical culture, genetic transmission or divine instruction—is a question as complicated as the human mind itself.

When we assess how much national character influences us and others, we must consider the fact that we come to that knowledge (at least in part) through our experience of the world. The truth reveals itself as we encounter the world and we consequently internalise that truth and embody it, through trusting and mistrusting, believing and disbelieving, loving and being indifferent, welcoming and fearing. Our everyday lives depend on instant judgements of instinct derived from internalised truths founded on experience.

Not infallible, not universal, not applicable in all circumstances, the powerful drives of instinct, impulse, aversion, attraction, and other core responses, allow us to survive, in the same way (in situations of danger) we flinch, duck, fall, reach out, shield, punch and protect instantly, without consideration. These reactions can lead to avoidable injury and death, but they more often save us (and others) from worse harm. In the same way, national character traits do seem to "work" in the environments and in the societies in which they arose. An evolutionary psychologist might describe national traits as an extended phenotype, which bonds individuals, strengthens society and aids transmission of the group's genes. In their natural habitats, the sub-verbal animal learns by imitation and by use of intelligence how to solve problems; it also follows innate instincts to survive, hunt, reproduce and raise offspring. This is not a justification for unwavering adherence to ideas about national character traits: it is simply an acknowledgement that such traits exist and have value. Perhaps, when we consider the logician's "naturalistic fallacy"—namely, that if an argument relies upon truth conforming to nature (or, more widely, the current status quo) then that argument lacks logic—we should pause and recognise the implicit presumption that men should seek to set themselves above and outside nature (and, implicitly, tradition). Perhaps, we could say, the logician seeks to demand of tradition proof of its validity for his approval or correction, and that scepticism about the existence and validity of national (or ethnic, regional, racial) character is an assertion that logic should surmount nature. Whether logic does (or should or can) take precedence over natural patterns is another discussion.

In a speech I delivered in the summer of 2022, I described how one comes to know the world through action:

> The reactionary creator follows his instinct, hardly different to those of a huntsman. When he works, he gains an intuitive understanding of his tools and his materials. He knows how the blade will twist in his hand, he can feel the grain of wood in the log, he knows the ring of true stone and clank of flawed stone when he raps it. I know how the paint will lie as I apply it and I could only know that through intuiting, with intuition the result of experience. These are the emergence of hidden truths that are uncovered by tutorship, experience, observation. This is internalised as a kind of muscle memory, which links him with his ancestors, a profound instinct that has a poetry to which men respond. [...] A craftsman will tell you that types of woods are not made equal and that the blunt blade is not only a danger to the wielder, it is an insult to the wood, it is slander to the tradition. The worker knows there has never been equality between men, between men and women, between animals and men, between any things in the world. He knows it because he lives it.[3]

Our lives depend on us recognising perennial truths that do not match what is presented to us as the truth by our teachers, politicians, priests, and other figures of authority. This essay suggests that there are ways of knowing the world and people—through action, through experience, through contemplation, through art-making—and that our instincts can reveal to us truths that we unconsciously knew but which outside authorities prefer to obscure or refute. We find these truths also through responding to art and literature. The struggle to reconcile these truths with our personal values and the civic values of our time is the struggle of nationalism and Romanticism.

*AA*

*September 2022*

# ENDNOTES

All online references retrieved August-September 2022.

1    See also numerous book and exhibitions published by me over the years, also the livestream discussions of art on the Ferro YouTube channel, https://www.youtube.com/channel/UCnQ04NWvy-j47g-0BNRsZew/featured.

2    See especially Thomas Sowell, *Discrimination and Disparities*, Basic Books, New York, 2019 (second edition).

3    Speech delivered in August 2022, to be published in Scyldings Events (*ed.*), *Logos and Praxis*, Coventry, 2022. See also Heidegger, "The Origin of the Work of Art", regarding *technitēs* and understanding truth through action.

# ROMANTICISM AND THE NORTHERN CHARACTER

*"There is no art without nationality", as Turgenev said some-where. True, that art is good and is well understood which draws on its national roots and which springs from the very heart of the nation. No artificial encouragement can create healthy art, no academies, no artistic genius is capable of creating it—or a teacher of nourishing the artist's talent—in the right way.*

Ilya Repin, 1893[1]

The recent exhibition[2] of the paintings of the Norwegian Symbolist artist Edvard Munch (1863–1944) showed Munch as a painter of the human essence, dealing with recurrent eternal themes: love, desire, loss, grief, fear, wonder. This is pretty much the standard approach for the artist—not least because of his Frieze of Life project, which conceived of life in such terms—but is no less true or important for us than it was for the first viewers, when we stand before Munch's great art. The Frieze of Life (conceived 1889, first exhibited 1902) was a series of paintings which would portray the progress of life for a person, presented in tableaux from different stages, incidents, or situations in a life. This included *Sphinx (Woman Three Stages)*, *At the Deathbed*, *Evening on Karl Johan Street*, *Jealousy*, *Melancholy*, *Anxiety*, *Ashes*, *Madonna*, *Puberty*, *The Lonely Ones*, *Despair*, *The Kiss*, *The Voice*, *The Dance of Life*, *Separation*, and *The Scream* (all 1892–1900). The marked paintings were included in the exhibition *Edvard Munch: Masterpieces from Bergen*.

Munch's Frieze of Life was both universal and personal,[3] being drawn from some of his own experiences of eternally recurring situations. *At the Deathbed* (1895) was a rendering of the death of his sister Sophie, in

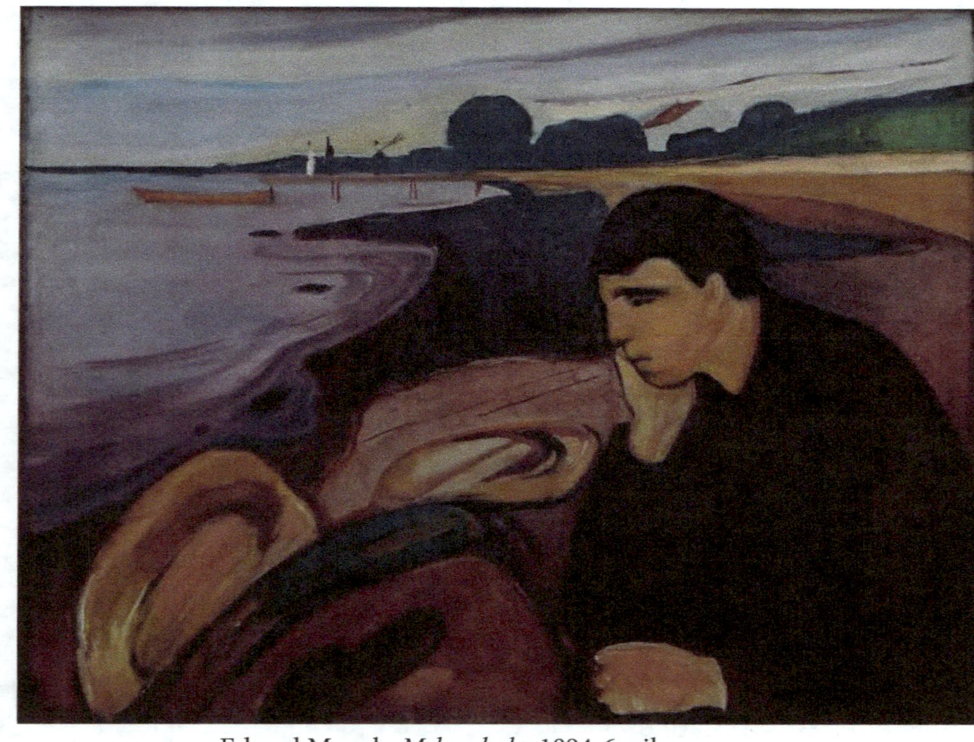

Edvard Munch, *Melancholy*, 1894-6, oil on canvas

1877, which itself echoed the death of their mother in 1868. The stark twist of verity is in the shadows cast by the unseen lamp at the head of the bed. Munch's observations of the complicated and turbulent private lives of associates in bohemian circles of Christiania and Berlin gave him ample material for paintings on the subject of despair and jealousy, including instances of suicide, murder, and infidelity. *Man and Woman* (1898) shows a man slumped in despair under the gaze of a nude woman, positioned above him. In Munch's world, the woman is supreme, the decider, slayer of men. She can withhold or divert her favours, rendering the male suitor pathetic or redundant. Munch has been seen as a misogynist. If he is so—and there is a case for that reading—he sees women with the power to be fickle and decide the fate of men of the highest calibre. ("Woman, who at one and the same time can be a saint, a whore and unhappily devoted."[4]) The artist's own private life provided enough drama for several lifetimes of autobiographical art. Munch's affairs and break-ups—including an incident where a mistress shot one of his fingers—were proof of the recurrence of suffering due to carnal passion and man's susceptibility to the eternal temptress. His *Death of Marat* (1907, not exhibited) shows Munch lying on a bloodied bed, assassinated by his lover Tulla Larsen who faces us nude, indomitable and proud. Munch was following an anarchist-bohemian manifesto written in Christiania that included one commandment that read, "Thou shalt write thy life."[5]

As the catalogue authors point out, Munch's personal psychodrama is definitely presented to position the artist in the starkest of situations, exploiting the actual events and weaving into them myth and history to elevate the art. We should not see this exaggeration as egotism but instead as the desire to make art that rises to the heroism of the greatest works in the canon. Munch serves his art, even if that means showing himself as more pitiable and weaker than he was. He is an actor in a stage play of his own life, where he plays himself. In this performance, Munch makes situations clearer than they were, gesturing emphatically and condensing action into symbolic tableaux. This emphatic power— found so distinctively in the heavy outlines, assertive painterliness and simplicity of forms—is one aspect that has contributed to the definition of Munch as a proto-Expressionist, if not the first Expressionist (along with Vincent Van Gogh). His forceful style was admired by many following artists, including Pablo Picasso and Francis Bacon.

In the exhibition and catalogue, Munch moves from early Impressionist-inflected realism (defiance of art conventions, in order to describe living reality) towards Symbolism, which presented an ur-reality, that primordial truth that exists below surfaces. (In that respect, Munch is very similar to Van Gogh.) Munch's aim was to be truthful about the unchanging realities of the lives of men and women by dispensing with anecdote, qualification and specificity.[6] His dramas of eternal man and eternal woman (not forgetting eternal child) have much in common with Romanticism and that movement's drive to set aside convention, religion and public morals to uncover enduring primordial truths. Romanticism, the intellectual and artistic forerunner of Symbolism, rejected the recent accretions of social and religious understanding of behaviour and the self, in order to find hidden things within human nature. This is, of course, as much an extension of Enlightenment science and philosophy as it is a refutation of it. Burke's examination of the physiological dimensions of our responses to stimuli beautiful or sublime, was an assertion of the value (and application) of biological science and nascent psychological investigation. We shall come back to the ideas of Romanticism later.

Munch's landscapes tend to avoid the picturesque, featuring views of beaches rather than mountains. We see meditative figures in profile rather than viewed from behind, contemplating the sea in calm summer evenings. The weather is generally undramatic. In *Starry Night* (1922–4), the infinity of the night sky is not so much undercut as emphasised by the prosaic shadow of the artist stretching over the snowy lawn, cast by an electric light behind him. Munch incorporated the weather as a component of his art, by leaving paintings outside to weather in rain, snow, and sun, subtly and unpredictably staining the canvases.

The catalogue[7] documents closely the actions of wealthy collector Rasmus Meyer (1858–1916), who personally knew Munch and bought work directly from his studio with the express intention of building a permanent collection that would be maintained after the death of collector and artist. The catalogue describes different cases of how patronage established handsome collections of the best art by certain exceptional artists and how there were left as legacies to inform compatriots' understanding and taste. It is fair to say that Munch's art has lodged deeply in the mental landscape of Scandinavians and the wider population, which responds to the memorable and assertive images. The images have a hold over us, even if we are not inhabitants of Norway, even if we have not seen the reflection of the moon on the fjord or the sun shining at midnight. The reverence for Munch's achievement is not least due to the commitment of Norwegian collectors, who saw Munch as an exponent of the new modern school and a demonstration that newly-independent Norway was a country capable of contribut-

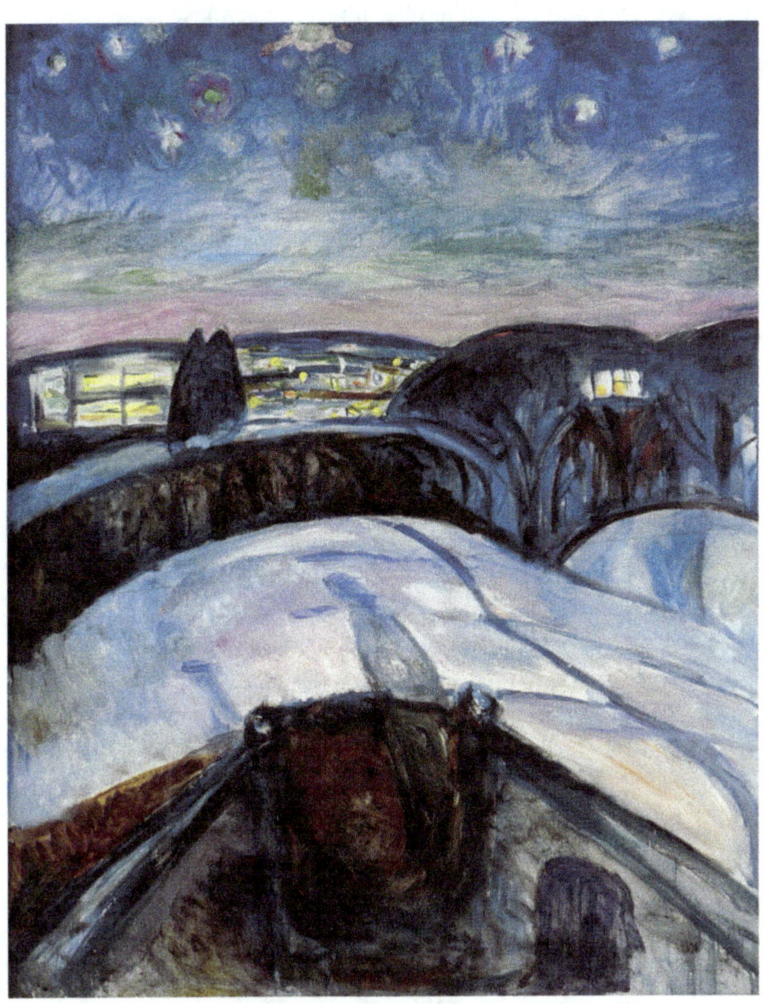

Edvard Munch, *Starry Night*, 1924, oil on canvas

ing art to the larger current of European culture. The establishing of such collections and maintaining their independence are issues fraught with problems. As we have seen from the cases of traducement of the collections of Barnes and Burrell, the wishes of benefactors are there to be spurned. Even when written into codicils and regulations that are explicitly opposed to the altering of collections, these demands are actively subverted by trustees, assisted by lawyers, financiers and politicians.[8] Thankfully, that has not been the case of Meyer's Munch collection.

Another exhibition which raised issues of the importance of place and people to the Romantic movement and its ideals was *Dreams of Freedom: Romanticism in Russia and Germany*.[9] The exhibition covered art by German, Russian, and Scandinavian artists working in the Romantic idiom, mostly with links to Dresden. The period selected is from 1800 to the 1890s. It is reviewed here from the catalogue.

At the turn of the nineteenth century, there was a mania for German stories, verse, painting, music and philosophy among intellectuals, social liberals, and Romantics in Russia. Germany appeared a model for intellectual refinement and imaginative exploits, with Dresden being the city held in highest esteem. The catalogue has a chronology of connections between Russians and Germans in Dresden during the nineteenth century. This includes military and diplomatic events during the Napoleonic Wars, when Russian troops defeated Napoleon (and his Saxon allies) at the Battle of Kulm. Dresden was a crossroads for Mitteleuropa and functioned as a site for mingling of German and Russian painters. For cultural tourists of the age—not least those on the Grand Tour—went to Dresden for its architecture (as "Florence on the Elbe") and its picture gallery (which contained Raphael's *Sistine Madonna* (1512–3). Local artists and the academy were poorly regarded in the first decade of the nineteenth century. Matters improved when Caspar David Friedrich (1774–1840) was appointed a member of the academy in 1816, though the consensus was that many of the Dresden painters were derivative.

The French Revolution of 1789 radically broke lines of continuation by destroying the status of the Church and king, replacing them with the Cult of the Supreme Being and democracy (or at least rule of the non-noble). The shackles of convention had been shattered.

> Artists and men of letters, such as monks, formed fraternities, devoting themselves to the ultimate goal, extolling the spiritual unity of artistic and religious revelation. Divine providence was replaced by a new kind of creator: the

artist, the writer, the poet and the musician who conjured up worlds of their own. Art replaced religion, museums replaced temples, theatrical productions replaced holy mass, and music became the complete embodiment of the world's divine harmony.[10]

For the Romantic, all seemed possible, from the expression of imaginative freedom to escape from religious oversight and the reshaping of society.[11] Romantic utopians took this as an opportunity to enact revolutionary aspirations.[12] For residents of Dresden, this would (eventually) culminate in the May 1849 republican uprising in Saxony against the king, an attempt inspired by the Europe-wide attempted revolutions of the preceding year.[13] The twin beliefs of (on one hand) the sanctity and worth of the individual outside of the collective and (on the other hand) the importance of universal brotherhood and communal action underpinned Romanticism, indicating its humanist and anti-theist character. Many Romantics considered themselves Christian but their other preoccupations and ideas meant that this Christianity was not conventional in character. This is a subject larger than can be treated here.

In the catalogue and exhibition, Friedrich is the towering presence. He was admired in his time by many.[14] Grand Duke Nikolai Pavlovich (future Czar Nicholas I) bought paintings from Friedrich's studio when he visited Dresden, and today there are nine paintings by him in the Hermitage. (Apparently other paintings by Friedrich in Russia were lost or destroyed during the early twentieth century.) Friedrich's symbolic landscapes—constructed from nature studies with added figures, buildings and subject to exaggeration and adaptation—are seen as pictorial poetry and as religious allegory.[15] His paintings were considered examples of the national genius of the German people, especially by the nationalists in later eras.[16] What does Romanticism in art mean, especially in German painting as embodied in the canvases of Friedrich?

> [A] heightened sensitivity to the natural world, combined with a belief in nature's correspondence to the mind; a passion for the equivocal, the indeterminate, the obscure and the faraway (objects shrouded in fog, a distant fire in the darkness, mountains merging with clouds, etc.); a celebration of subjectivity bordering on solipsism, often coupled with a morbid desire that that self be lost in nature's various infinities; an infatuation with death; valorization of night over day, emblematizing a reaction against Enlightenment

and rationalism; a nebulous but all-pervading mysticism; and a melancholy, sentimental longing or nostalgia which can border on kitsch.[17]

This is the subject matter and style of Romantic painting; the ideas were shared by novelists, poets and philosophers. Of the philosophers, one thinks of Edmund Burke's discussions of terrifying sublimity, and of the following description from Immanuel Kant:

> Bold, overhanging, and, as it were, threatening rocks, thunderclouds piled up the vault of heaven, borne along with flashes and peals, volcanos in all their violence of destruction, hurricanes leaving desolation in their track, the boundless ocean rising with rebellious force, the high waterfall of some mighty river [...][18]

Here is Friedrich's reported comment on the nebulous:

> When a landscape is covered in fog, it appears larger, more sublime, and heightens the strength of the imagination and excites expectation, rather like a veiled woman. The eye and fantasy feel themselves more attracted to the hazy distance than to that which lies near and distinct before us.[19]

This was at a time—after the violent caesurae of the republican, anti-clericalist French Revolution and the American War of Independence showed that the organising principles of states did not have to be grounded in crown or religion—when national identity was becoming increasingly important. Old empires were split into nations, principalities, bishoprics and duchies, which were consecutively absorbed into larger states; the old glue of feudal structures and regional trading networks was dissolved, as we see the rise of the nation state. Loyalty was no longer a chain of mutual duties in a strict hierarchy culminating in a monarch or prince of the Church; it became a collective project of an ethnic folk organised under the authority of a centralised and unified government, with a group cause being self-determination, and the incorporation into one state of the lands settled by kinsmen.

Friedrich and the Norwegian landscape painter Johan Christian Dahl (1788–1855) (a friend and colleague of Friedrich's in Dresden, whose work also features in the exhibition) became more themselves and better embodiments of their nations when separated from their homelands, it was said.

In Romanticism, the idea of homeland arises out of a loss. It was not until they were in foreign lands that leading artists discovered how their identity was shaped by their origins. In Dresden, Friedrich, who hailed from Pomerania, was seen as northern German—not only in his choice of subjects, such as the Baltic Sea and megalithic tombs, but also on account of his demure and withdrawn demeanour. It was not until he was in Rome that Johan Christian Dahl developed into a painter of harsh Norwegian nature.[20]

National character is understood comparatively. The paintings of Friedrich are full of travellers and observers briefly inhabiting unpopulated places. The coasts, cliffs, mountains, forests and ruins are not places where one lives: rather, they are places one encounters the dramatic, ineffable, and sublime. The tomb of prehistoric man allows modern man to reflect on the human condition of mortality. The theme and iconography are as important as the appearance of the picture.[21] On viewing Friedrich's landscapes, we are reminded of distance, travel, and dislocation. Thus, the Romanticism of Friedrich at once reminds the viewer of his connections to the place where he is temporally, and the place whence he comes and belongs.

The exhibition documented multiple connections between German and Russian Romanticism, with the direction of influence coming from Germany towards Russian artists and collectors. The selection of Friedrich paintings, not least from Russian museums, was excellent, and it was engrossing to see these paintings reproduced so large and clear. Carl Gustav Carus (1789–1869) is a great and devoted disciple of Friedrich. His motifs and approach are similar to Friedrich's—figures on a boat, wanderers in wild landscapes in moonlight, mountain views—but his handling is much simpler, flatter, and less crisp. When he attempts the more dramatic—a stormy sea, closer to the art of Dahl—he does not fully succeed. It is hard to see Carus as more than a poor man's Friedrich, at least on this showing.

Carl Blechen (1798–1840) is more original and intense. *Gothic Church Ruins* (1826) shows a figure asleep in a church (or cathedral) not so much overtaken by nature but fused with natural terrain. The floor of the building is a rocky brook, worn through the now-exposed crypt. Saplings emerge from stone parapets, echoing the slender mullions of the Gothic windows below—a beautiful piece of visual rhyme. The ruin was a staple of fine art and literature made by the Romantics. The work of nature and of man is fused in the ruin. Man's architecture is altered by the forces of nature and the passage of time, presenting the observer with a representation which reminds him of the limits of man's abilities.

This confrontation between man, nature, and time is at the heart of the
Romantic aesthetic, which attributes less to God, assigning the cosmos
to forces which are not necessarily divine. Awe is generated by contemplation of the mighty sublime. The Romantic aesthetic also includes the
advancement of artistic ideas concerning melancholy, grief, morbidity,
dissolution, decay, entropy, and disease. Blechen's dramatic landscapes
and building paintings in oil and ink-wash are richly satisfying, and he
can be classed at the second rank, just below Friedrich and Dahl.

The Nazarene movement was represented by Edward von Steinle
(1810–1886), Wilhelm Schadow (1789–1862) and Johann Friedrich
Overbeck (1789–1869). Their weaknesses in handling and painterly
presence are apparent in the selected examples; notwithstanding the
deliberate archaism of the Nazarene movement, these are stiff and flat
as paintings. The portraits seem notably weaker than the landscapes.
Ferdinand Hartmann (1774–1842) is a curiosity. He is not a natural
painter. His modelling of figures and drapery is crude, his lighting is
rudimentary, his composition lacks nuance and sophistication, and
we have no sense of inhabiting the pictorial space. Yet, his two images
here—a kneeling woman holding a dish; death as a skeleton stealing
children from a sleeping mother's bed—are impressively memorable
and bold, perhaps precisely because they are so direct (even naïve) as
paintings. He accomplishes the tableaux because (rather than despite)
being so limited as a technician. The force of his images strikes precisely
because we are not delighted by the inventiveness of the drapery or
preoccupied by fine execution. Romantic painter Philipp Otto Runge
(1777–1810) is represented by a self-portrait and his *Times of Day* print
series, which has always seemed to me (in previous viewings) rather
chilly and meretricious—the opposite of Hartmann, you could say.

Much better are the landscapes and ruin paintings of Ernst Ferdinand Oehme (1797–1855). *Cathedral in Winter* (1821) is a nocturne
of worshippers arriving for an evening service on a snowy night at a
Gothic Cathedral; the only warm hues being those of the light within
the building, indicating the salvation and comfort afforded by Christian worship. Dahl was famous for his nocturnes, and *View of Dresden*
(1839) is one of his finest. It shows Dresden's famous skyline, with
shredded clouds obscuring a full moon, silvery reflections on the river
brighter than the few paltry lights of a fire or lamp. It reminds one of
what has been taken from us by the saturation of artificial illumination
in not only our cities but suburbs, industrial outskirts, and motorways.
There is something humbling and inducive of meditative contemplation
about observing a landscape by moonlight. The provision of indiscrim-

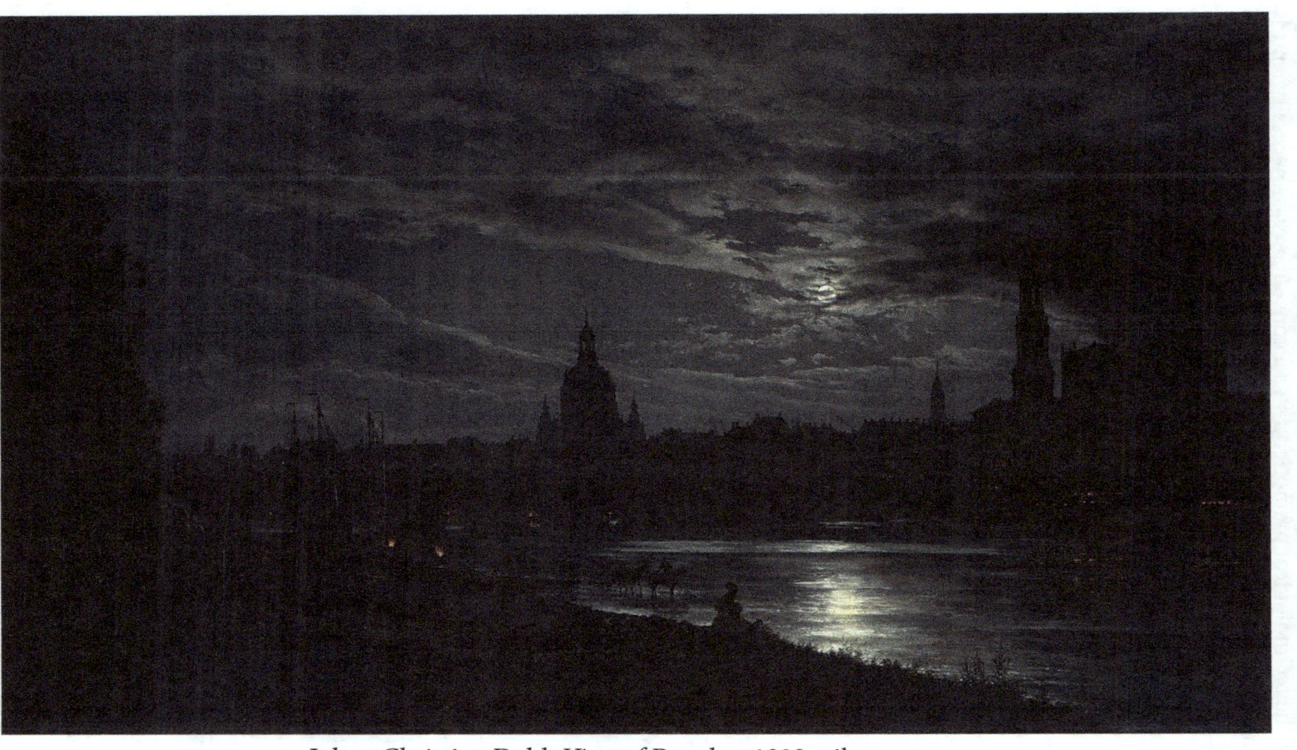

Johan Christian Dahl, *View of Dresden*, 1839, oil on canvas

inate artificial lighting seems as much of an intrusion—a manifestation of the technological panopticon—as a convenience or necessity, and is one that distances us from our ancestors. For contrast, compare it to Bernardo Bellotto's daylight view of the city.[22]

The cover of the catalogue features a detail from Maksim Nikiforovich Vorobyov's *Oak, Shattered by Lightning (Thunderstorm)* (1842), which shows a tree cleft in two by a curving lightning bolt. Yet the detail does not do the drama of the picture—or the daring of its painter—its due. That motif takes up barely half the painting and is located on the right side; the left side is almost blank—a haze of waves whipped to spume and a distance flicker of lighting from a murky sky. It is extremely audacious. However, it would not be accurate to state that the most striking works here are entirely from Russians, but these paintings will be barely known by even connoisseurs of Romantic art in the West. Vorobyov is one of the finds of the exhibition, for a Westerner.

The painting of Alexander Andreyevich Ivanov (1806–1858) was given a prominent presence in this exhibition. It is ironic that the most striking piece by him is a half-length seated *Portrait of Vittoria Marini* (late 1840s) rather than his mythological or religious scenes. The spatial ambiguity of the sitter's left hand is the most noteworthy aspect. The hand seems to rest on the cheek, yet anatomical understanding and absence of shadows from the head suggest the hand is not touching the cheek. It is quite a curious solution to the pictorial problem: thus, the hand seems to be both touching the cheek and to be held forward. It is quite close in atmosphere, approach, palette, and handling to the paintings of the 1920s and 1930s by Lotte Laserstein (1898–1993). Grand claims[23] are made for Aleksei Gavrilovich Venetsianov (1780–1847) but they are not borne out by this selection. Only the very simple and warm-hued *Harvesting. Summer* (mid-1820s)—showing a seated peasant resting from harvest, light falling on her back—is enchanting and fresh. His portraits of peasants range from the touching to the trite.

Of the Russians, we get none of the Peredvizhniki (Передви́жники, Russian: Wanderers) movement. Enthusiasts will sorely miss their grandeur and intensity. Ivan Aivazovsky (1817–1900) is very poorly served by one lacklustre marine. He was the greatest of the Russian Empire's painters of the period. Was he largely omitted because he was a painter of seascapes, and also an ethnic Armenian? There is no dearth of wonderful paintings by him in Russian museums. Was he too difficult to integrate into the narrative? This is a shame because Aivazovsky is a painter who should be exhibited and discussed more often, although he is better known in Germany than elsewhere in Europe.

There is a section of the exhibition catalogue covering the oil sketches commonly made by landscape painters in this age. Such small sketches were made by artists *en plein air* on location and then used as the backgrounds for more finished studio works, usually involving figures and extraneous themes, such as mythological or Biblical subjects. These works have often been lost, and the use of card and paper as cheap portable supports has led to the deterioration of the pictures. A particularly fine collection of oil-on-paper landscape sketches (many made by artists visiting the Mediterranean) is held by the National Museum of Wales, Cardiff. The contemporary taste for the small, roughly finished, and non-narrative means that there is now a ready audience for these paintings whereas at the time they were made, they were considered studio materials.

The exhibition gathered material relating to Dresden's most famous painting, Raphael's *Sistine Madonna*. The painting was bought by Frederick Augustus II in 1754. It was not considered a major work at the time and only subsequently became famous with its relocation to Dresden and temporary exhibition in Berlin. Numerous notable (as well as ordinary) people made a pilgrimage to the Dresdner Gemäldegalerie to view it. Artists came to admire and copy.[24] Apparently, it was more common to see the painting in the gallery attended by at least one copyist than it was to see it without any. The catalogue reproduces some of the many German and Russian copies and illustrates watercolours of stately interiors that housed full-size copies. Both Dostoyevsky[25] and Tolstoy had copies of the painting in their homes, although Tolstoy later became averse to Raphael, whose perfection began to seem intolerable.

# ENDNOTES

1    Repin, 5 November 1893, in Harrison, 1998, pp. 923–4.

2    *Edvard Munch: Masterpieces from Bergen*, 27 May–5 September 2022, Courtauld Gallery, London.

3    "[…] I stood before the pictures of Edvard Munch; once again I found myself confronted with the naked revelation of an individuality, with the creative products of a somnambular and transcendental consciousness, what is commonly called 'the unconscious'. […] For me this individuality is what is immortal and inalienable. It is the fundamental stock or trunk, upon which new properties and characteristics are continually engrafted through the process of heredity, indeed it is what sustains this process; this is an individuality which eternally perpetuates itself and has been living on continuously ever since the primal beginning, since the incipient dawning of life […]" Stanislaw Przybyszewski, "Psychic Naturalism (The Work of Edvard Munch)", 1894, in Harrison, 1998, p. 1045. Przybyszewski was a friend of Munch when they lived in Berlin.

4    Munch, quoted in Wright, 2022, p. 109.

5    Prideaux, 2005, ch. 9.

6    Munch, 1909: "Just as Leonardo da Vinci studied the recesses of the human body and dissected cadavers, I try to dissect souls." Quoted in Prideaux, 2005, p. 110.

7    Wright, 2022.

8    See in particular my review of the Museum Mayer van den Bergh, Bruges for an example of a museum that has resisted subversion, https://alexanderadamsart.wordpress.com/2021/08/08/museum-mayer-van-den-berghe-a-conservative-vision-of-past-and-future/.

9    *Dreams of Freedom: Romanticism in Russia and Germany*, 22 April-8 August 2021, State Tretyakov Gallery, Moscow, 2 October 2021–6 June 2022, Staatliche Kunstammlungen Dresden.

10    Sergey Fofanov in *Dreams of Freedom*, 2022, p. 54.

11    "Art raises its head where the religions relax their hold […] so that the feelings expelled from the sphere of religion by the Enlightenment throw themselves into art; in individual cases into political life as well, indeed even straight into the sciences." Nietzsche, *Human, All Too Human*, quoted in *Dreams of Freedom*, 2022, p. 144.

12    See Friedrich Schlegel on the French Revolution, in Harrison, 2000, p. 908.

13    "In chronological terms the Romantic era is generally bookended by two key dates—1789 and 1848. In the space of less than sixty years—a period that

saw the French Revolution, the Napoleonic Wars and the sequence of bourgeois revolutions which swept across Europe in the mid-nineteenth century – the whole world order changed dramatically." Sergey Fofanov, *Dreams of Freedom*, p. 73.

14    For contemporary praise and criticism of Friedrich, see texts by Friedrich Ramdohr, Clemens Brentano, Kleist and (indirectly) Friedrich himself, all in Harrison, 2000.

15    "The focus of the Romantics was not on topographically exact view of a landscape." Holger Birkholz, *Dreams of Freedom*, pp. 89–90.

16    "The landscape painter Caspar David Friedrich, for example, is far more important in German painting than any of the historical painters of his time […]" Golomstock, 1990, p. 288.

17    Koerner, 2009, ch. 3.

18    Immanuel Kant, *Critique of Pure Judgement*, 1790.

19    Vaughan, 2004, p. 257.

20    Holger Birkholz, *Dreams of Freedom*, 2022, pp. 89–90.

21    "A painter should not merely paint what he sees in front of him, he should paint what he sees within himself. If he sees nothing within, he should not paint what he sees before him …" Friedrich, quoted in *Dreams of Freedom*, 2022, p. 146.

22    *Dresden viewed from the Right Bank of the Elbe below the Augustusbrücke* (1748), Gemäldegalerie Alte Meister, Dresden.

23    "[…] Venetsianov's œuvre is one of the most radiant and harmonious among the masters of Russian art." Svetlana Stepanova, *Dreams of Freedom*, 2022, p. 164 .

24    For Philipp Otto Runge's admiration of *The Sistine Madonna*, see Runge in Harrison, 2000, pp. 979–980.

25    "In his novel *Demons*, Dostoyevsky foresaw the imminent destruction of the Romantic about *The Sistine Madonna*. The next generation of literary giants began to ridicule and cynically vilify the ideal of beauty and spirituality that had been cultivated in the recent past." Lyudmila Markina, *Dreams of Freedom*, p. 138. Consider this point in relation to assaults on ideas of normative beauty by political radicals of the twentieth century and most importantly in recent years, especially in connection with the canon.

# ROMANTICISM FROM THE ENLIGHTENMENT AGAINST THE ENLIGHTENMENT

The core pillars of Romanticism are freedom (from tradition and religion), nature (submission to it as a key determinant of man and civilisation), individualism (the search of the interior character), and emotion (subjectivity as universal and a key principle for human comprehension of the world). Holger Birkholz notes as key concepts in Romanticism freedom, nature, pre-history, mysticism, night, irony and universal poetry.[1] To this we can add the strange and mysterious, spontaneity[2], imagination, and originality. "What attracts most is the unknown. The well-known has no further attraction. The power of perception is in itself the greatest of charms."[3] Self-absorption is a legacy of Enlightenment philosophical investigations of the mind and personality. We can say that the unknown includes the aberrant, grotesque, and macabre. The art of Henry Fuseli and other Romantics dwell on phenomena of dreams, madness and the demonic; it was the subject matter of Gothic fiction. The dramatic ruin and processes of decay—not least decay of the human body—elicited the sublime response and touched areas of deep feeling, which confounded the rationalism of the Enlightenment and symbolised the frailty of man and civilisation before the might of nature. Romantics asserted that logic and science did not explain mysteries of the world and the human heart. The horror genre derives from Gothic tales and pictures, although elements of horror can be found as far back as ancient myths.

The rise of Romanticism comes as an outgrowth of—and a reaction against—Enlightenment thinking. Enlightenment empiricism undermined the foundations of traditionalism and Christianity through the scientific method, which opened up a space for the adventurous creator to turn to mythology and pre-history. Political liberalism centred the idea of individuality—both as civic principle and a field for personal exploration—which encouraged a rejection of traditional morality and community action, in favour of subjective morality and pursuit of individual self-knowledge. However, Romanticism was in some respects counter-Enlightenment in its emphasis on emotionality and subjectivity over metaphysics, primeval atavism over incremental progressivism, paganism over atheism and a rejection of industrialisation in favour of craft. Romanticism took as its site of deepest contemplation and source of truth the rural—and even better, the untamed wilds—in a deliberate rejection of the expanding towns and cities. Wordsworth famously discovered the transcendental within by observing himself react to the world, but he did reach such an insight whilst standing atop a mountain pass rather than looking across a town square. The transcendental may come from within, but the stimulus is often the sublime or remarkable. Romantics sought to expose the unseen correspondences through art.

> For the Symbolists as for the Romantics, the world of art was the only true world, which the visionary artist-adventurer explored with the intuitive powers of his imagination that enabled him to perceive the hidden relationships between the visible and the invisible. These correspondences were embodied in the magical symbols, whose function was the same as that of the Romantic image: to express the inexpressible, to mediate the artist's private perception of the transcendental.[4]

A fundamental contradiction within Romanticism is its expression of a naturally aristocratic temperament whilst positing an egalitarian attitude towards the value of man. While Romanticism in some respects backed the universalism of Enlightenment political thought, which saw no distinction in terms of class status among men as regards ability, capacity and worth, Romantics venerated the free man. The free man was capable of fulfilling his potential, provided time and opportunity for education and cultivation of taste. While this was theoretically open to all non-serfs, it was most usually the domain of the aristocrat, who was liberated by opportunity. As David Hume pointed out on in his essay on taste, only a few in society had the chance to develop cultivated taste through exposure to education and experience. It was the man who had developed his taste, recognised his own character through reflection and had chosen to risk all in action who was the ultimate embodiment of Romantic Man. Romanticism also adulated the man of action, one who was (in the case of Byron) able to afford travel to a foreign land to fight in a war of ideals. Critically, it was the Romantic man who came to action through free will who was the greatest of heroes, not the man who was forced through circumstances to defend his family, kin, and faith. It was often the man of noble character (rather than of noble birth) who was held up as an ideal, who may have risen through his natural qualities to distinguished rank. There seems an ambivalence among Romantics towards what would become called the Great Man theory of history.

The Romantics believed in heroic action but deprecated unearned social status; they talked in terms of the exceptional man of thought and action as the way-finder for mankind, while also advocating for the welfare of the common man. Even if there is no outright contradiction in these positions, it displays two separate areas of sympathy, not always complementary. It is commonly argued that the Romantics wished to portray the life of the ordinary man and elevate it to the realm of heroes. One social spur for the rise of Romanticism has been suggested.

> As Henri Brunswig has argued in his account of the social circumstances of Romanticism, it was from precisely the surplus of over-educated, highly ambitious, under-employed and deeply frustrated middle-class young men that the Romantic movement drew its members: 'The students thronging the universities are well aware of the difficulties ahead of them. This makes them more eager to attract attention to themselves. To become famous is a short cut to the heights of a career in politics or the civil service.'[5]

Just as the French Revolution was led by the intelligentsia, lawyers, writers, and university graduates frustrated by the impediments of court patronage and Church influence, so the Romantic movement was a set of counter-elites seeking to overturn the royal houses and Church of their lands, seeking to ally with the peasants and dispossessed in order to displace the incumbent governing elite.

Consider (as an example) the apparently egalitarian views of Romantic poet William Wordsworth (1770–1850). For him as a writer, country life and rustic subjects lent themselves to greater dignity in verse because they were more essential and less contaminated by false sophistication:

> [In rustic subjects] the essential passions of the heart find
> a better soil in which they can attain their maturity, are less

> under restraint, and speak a plainer and more emphatic language; because in that condition of life our elementary feelings co-exist in a state of greater simplicity, and, consequently, may be more accurately contemplated, and more forcibly communicated; because the manners of rural life germinate from those elementary feelings; and, from the necessary character of rural occupations, are more easily comprehended, and are more durable; and lastly, because in that condition the passions of men are incorporated with the beautiful and permanent forms of nature.[6]

Rural life had generated an authentic language (which was both vernacular and ancient) that poets should adopt, instead of shunning it for ostentatious artificiality. "Accordingly, such a language, arising out of repeated experience and regular feelings, is a more permanent, and a far more philosophical language, than that which is frequently substituted for it by Poets [...]"[7]

This veneration of the common man and his language is seen as an extension of the cult of egalitarianism[8], expounded by Enlightenment humanist thinkers, not least Jean-Jacques Rousseau, and found in the rhetoric of the French Revolution. Rousseau's ideas inverted the Christian conception of man born sinful and guided to salvation through following the teachings of Christ, replacing that with a conception of man born good and made evil through the inequities of property and society. This egalitarianism and rejection of original sin (as the foundation of social relations) led to the humanistic contradiction of the "Great Chain of Being", with men assigned their stations in life according to birth and circumstance, by instead offering a vision of position determined primarily by merit and self-determination.

Romanticism responded to the breaking of the Great Chain of Being (or duty) by celebrating an alternative chain: blood loyalty, specifically national and ancestral. Instead of duty linked to roles—employee, serf, apprentice, master, partner, tenant, congregant, co-religionist, father, husband, son—which may or may not have been hereditary or otherwise involuntary, Romantic thinkers sought out connections (notional or actual) with kinsmen present and past. This latter aspect foregrounded a fascination with ancestors and prehistory. This was specifically disassociated with religious ties and went back to a time before Christianity and the then-current ruling royal houses. There was a bond of blood that linked kinsmen together and back to their ancestors of prehistory. In art and literature, there came a wave of scenes of ancient history related to the native country rather than Hellenic

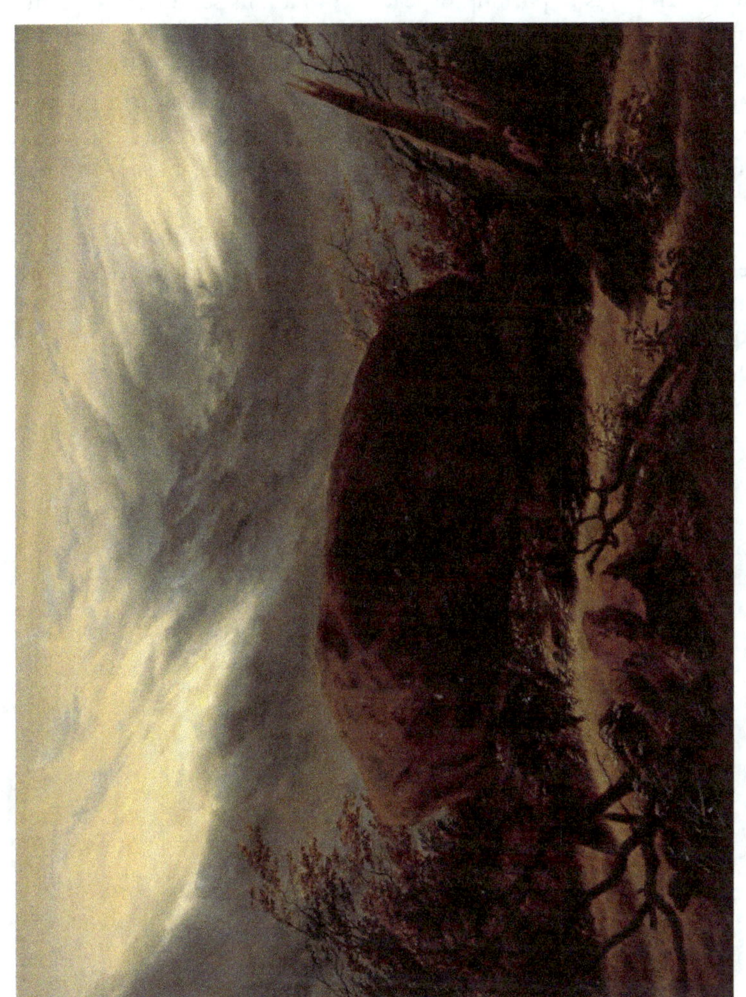

Caspar David Friedrich, *Dolmen in Autumn*, 1820, oil on canvas

or Roman history. The Enlightenment study of archaeology became a matter of national importance. Finding the truth of ancient people's origins—obscured or erased by the universalist Christian religion—became a project essential for the definition of nationhood and kin. The idea of blood bonds superseded many of the established bonds of loyalty. This was important for leaders of nations set on self-determination as new boundaries were formed and new institutions and laws had to be derived in lands no longer dominated by authority of Church and monarch. This is not only philosophically congruent with an age of Romanticism (as part of the Enlightenment) but also a necessity from an organisational point of view, in an epoch when established loyalties are suddenly weakened or severed.

Romantic poets meditated upon stone circles; Romantic painters depicted ancient burial mounds. Both are a sign of a new engagement with pre-Christian stage of civilisation. We find in the paintings of late Romantic English painter John Martin the figure of Merlin, the Welsh wizard who escaped English invaders.

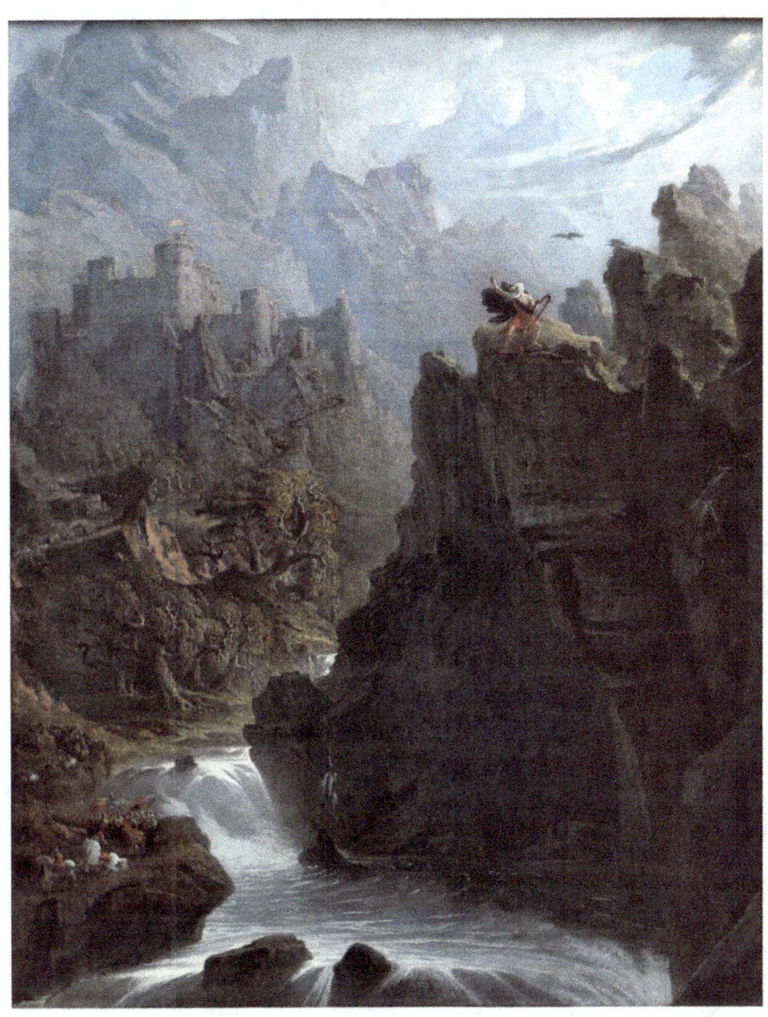

John Martin, *The Bard*, c. 1817, oil on canvas

# ENDNOTES


1    Holzer in *Dreams of Freedom*, 2022, pp. 23–33.

2    Furst, 1969, p. 78.

3    Novalis, "Fugitive Thoughts", 1798-1801 (?), in Harrison, 2000, p. 913.

4    Furst, 1969, p. 287.

5    Koerner, 2009, ch. 5.

6    William Wordsworth, "Preface", *The Lyrical Ballads*, 1801/1802, London.

7    *Ibid.*

8    "In spite of its lack of emphasis on individualism in its theories, the English Romantic movement is in practice most profoundly individualistic." Furst, 1969, p. 61.

# THE CULT OF
# THE PRIMITIVE

To gain an insight into the linkage between Romanticism and the investigation of prehistory in the pursuit of nation-binding myths, we can look at the case of the Ossian epic verse. Epic verses attributed to Ossian—an ancient Scottish warrior and clan leader, previously supposed to be a mythical character—were published in 1761 and 1763 by James Macpherson. He claimed he had transcribed and translated them from Gaelic oral recitations of poems conceived by Ossian. Here is a passage:

> Let vapour and gloom lie on Crona;
> Let them lie upon the king's path,
> Concealing his steps from my eyes;
> Evermore be the brave forgotten.
> Armed chiefs on the plain have no leader;
> Their steps are not heard round his steel.
> O Caruinn, Caruinn of floods!
> Wind thou with thy water in blood;
> The leader of men is in gloom.[1]

The German philosopher Johann Gottfried Herder (1744–1803)—like many—was captivated by what he read. He believed (as per Winckelmann, discussed later) that the character of society and environment had shaped the aesthetic sensibility of the poet. Here is Herder:

> Know then, that the more barbarous a people is—that is, the more alive, the more freely acting (for that is what the word means)—the more barbarous, that is, the more alive, the more free, the closer to the senses, the more lyrically dynamic its songs will be, if songs it has. The more remote a people is from an artificial, scientific manner of thinking,

speaking, and writing, the less its songs are made for paper and print, the less its verses are written for the dead letter. The purpose, the nature, the miraculous power of these songs as the delight, the driving-force, the traditional chant and everlasting joy of the people—all this depends on the lyrical, living, dance-like quality of the song, on the living presence of the images, and the coherence and, as it were compulsion of the content, the feelings; on the symmetry of the words and syllables, and sometimes even of the letters, on the flow of the melody, and on a hundred other things which belong to the living world, to the gnomic song of the nation, and vanish with it.[2]

The reception of the Ossian poems was divided, with some praising them as proof of Northern European genius. Heinrich von Kleist (1777–1811) acclaimed the poems of Ossian and Ludwig Gotthard Kosegarten as equivalent to the paintings of Friedrich.[3] Others denounced them as fake. When Macpherson presented the Ossian poems, he had specifically described Ossian as "the Homer of the North". Ossian could provide an aesthetic counterbalance to the Greek canon, offering a Gaelic-Celtic-Northern-European sensibility comparable in greatness to Homer. Herder believed this and in the poems' authenticity. As it turned out, the Ossian poems were hoaxes—or heartfelt imitations of an imagined Celtic verse—written by Macpherson, in an act that fused Romantic fantasy and Scottish nationalism.

This exposure did not matter for "'Ossianism' had preceded *Ossian*."[4] "And the Ossianic craze persisted well after the fraud had been exposed, for the simple reason that the mood or climate captured by the so-called 'Gaelic' bard responded to a deep aesthetic need."[5] Although Herder's praise of primitive cultures was based on a deception, admiration for pre-industrial societies was to become a persistent tenet of later aesthetics and movements. The articulation of the cult of the primitive is a critical development and something very different from Winckelmann's adulation of the Greeks. What Winckelmann lauded was great technical sophistication and cultivated expression of a lost advanced society. Herder's ideal was a vanished oral Celtic culture, with which (as a Teuton) he felt kinship, precisely because it was (a) not Mediterranean, (b) Northern, (c) *Völkisch* (German: folkish, of the folk) and not of a class-stratified society, and (d) unsophisticated. Herder would be seen as a central figure in the early history of German nationalism. Herder's search for Nordic culture was rooted in affinity for the German forest as a specific antipode to Winckelmann's classical ideal art from the hot treeless Greek isles.

The association between, on one hand, non-Western and seemingly ancient cultures and (on the other hand) the concept of raw, untutored power of expression has proved persistent. Paul Gauguin sought pre-Christian society in Tahiti; Max Pechstein travelled to Palau looking for a native culture uncontaminated by modernity. Eugène Delacroix (1798–1863) never travelled to the American frontier but used his imagination and ethnographic description to paint *The Natchez* (1834–5), a scene of Native Americans nurturing a new-born infant after escaping a massacre by French colonists. The nobility and tragic fatalism of the savage is held as heroic and an implicit reproof of the imperialism of modern Europeans. Denigrating Western culture as deracinated, effete, polluted, and inauthentic—in comparison to the primitive, both foreign and ancient—is commonplace in the age of Romanticism and afterwards. It is yoked to the idea of moral decadence and societal decline. There is frequently the call to revitalise the over-sophisticated civilisation through contact with (or emulation of) cultures with pre-modern agrarian values, understanding of nature and secret knowledge that are akin to, or actually, magical. Europeans defined themselves against the Oriental, as an avatar of simultaneous over-sophistication and historical anachronism.

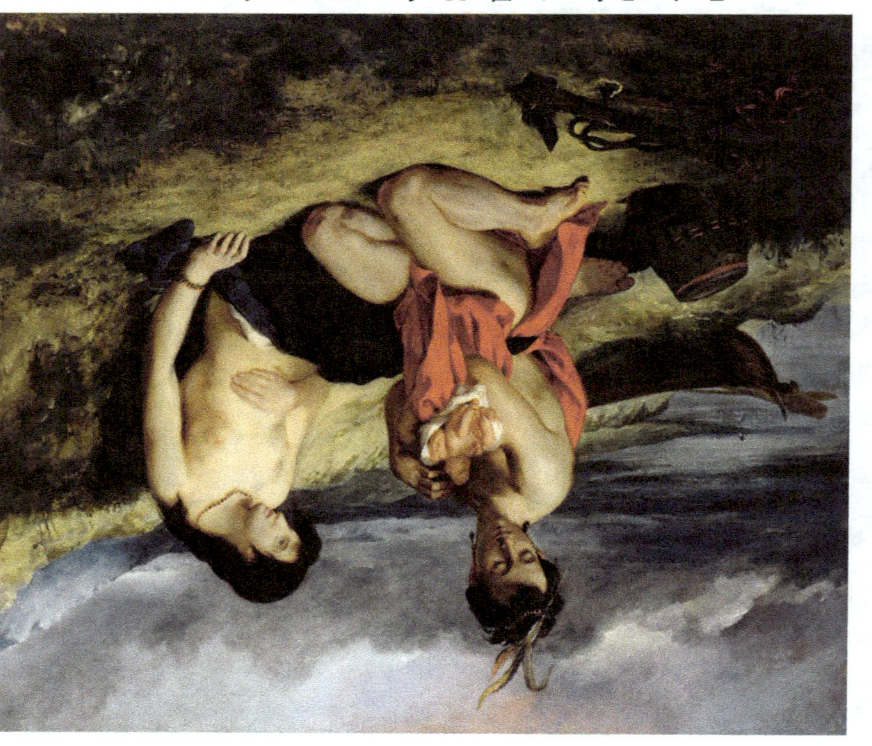

Eugène Delacroix, *The Natchez*, 1834–5, oil on canvas

ENDNOTES

1    Peter McNaughton, *The Poems of* Ossian, Blackwood & Sons, Edinburgh, 1887, p. 28, online: https://deriv.nls.uk/dcn6/7600/76001851.6.pdf.

2    Herder, 1773, quoted in Paul Guyer, *A History of Modern Aesthetics: Volume 1. The Eighteenth Century*, Cambridge University Press, Cambridge, 2018, pp. 386–7.

3    Kleist in Harrison, 2000, pp. 1031–2.

4    Clay, 1981, p. 6.

5    *Ibid.*

# ORIENTALISM
# AND NATIONALISM

The age of Orientalism began with Napoleon's campaign in Egypt (1798–1801), which incidentally provided fodder for Enlightenment anthropology and comparative theology. At this time, philology became an important branch of language scholarship, as academics used the study of word derivations and meanings to reconstruct paths of language and cultural transmission, and to map cross-continental migration. Discovery of the Rosetta Stone in 1799 led to the first interpretation of ancient Egyptian hieroglyphs. Orientalism became a foundational counterpart to philology; anthropologists used new discoveries in the Near East to confirm and disprove Biblical history. However scientific much of this work was, it was intimately tied to the observer's image of his own nation and assumptions about that nation's foundational myths, which reflected the Romantic and heroic origins that inspired pride among the people. Using observations of other nations, historians sought to confirm or debunk national myths of a Romantic character.

Painters took up Orientalist subjects—the hunt, the execution, the harem, the desert caravan, the faithful at prayer—in ways that blended the living reality of life in the Near and Middle East with that same region in the times of the ancients. It can be tricky to distinguish in paintings between scenes of Egypt in the times of the pharaohs and the Ottoman Empire—deliberately so, it seems. These depictions of the Orient were a means by which European Christians defined themselves against the Eastern (mainly Muslim) inhabitants of Asia and North Africa. The view of Orientals as existing at a lower, earlier stage of civilisation was a comparative measure and a staple of anthropological understanding of not just the course of humanity in general, but also of the West.

Orientalism derives from the scientism of Enlightenment and the Romantic scepticism about Christianity. It also ties into the European nationalist projects of the Napoleonic era, underpinned by the fear of the piratical Moor and the occupying Turk, mingled with admiration for the martial spirit of the Ottoman, the hardiness of the Bedouin, the beauty of the *houri* and the architectural wonders of ancient Assyria and Egypt. The constant friction between Christendom and the Muslim Ottoman Empire in the Balkans during the post-1683 period sharpened the differences between West and East. It would become a cause for Christians and Muslims globally. Byron died in Greece during the campaign for Greek independence from the Ottomans.

The Orientalist genre (ostensibly didactic and judgemental) allowed painter, poet, and historian licence to drench themselves in the glories and barbarities of the exotic East. Witness the Orientalist paintings of Ludwig Deutsch, Jean-Léon Gérôme, John Frederick Lewis, Jean-Étienne Liotard and others. Consider the blank verse play of Lord Byron *Sardanapalus* (1821), describing the downfall of the last king of Nineveh, which was subsequently painted by Delacroix, in 1827.

Assyria was being surveyed by European archaeologists in the period. History, archaeology, poetry, and painting became arms of the Romantic-Enlightenment Orientalist movement, which sought to enlighten and enchant, and the results of which were used to nationalist ends of defining the other, defining the self, understanding history, and justifying colonialism.

The anthropology of European explorers and colonisers allowed the extrapolation of conclusions about European peoples' origins following observations of non-Western societies, finding in them aspects to praise as well as condemn. There was much debate about the notion of the noble savage. The nobility and the ferocity of the American Indian, Maori and Hawaiian were feared and admired and those living peoples were compared to the Celts, Gauls, Franks, Vikings, and other ancient peoples of Europe. The taming of the untrammelled passions and rude customs of ancient European peoples, it was said by some, was both necessary for the progress of civilisation but also a lamentable diminishment.

The Battle of Teutoburg Forest, in 9 AD, was the defeat of a Roman army under Publius Quinctilius Varus by an alliance of German tribes under the command of Hermann, which took place in the heart of the German lands. The battle was taken up by German nationalists in the nineteenth century as an emblem of Germanic distinction, not least as it displayed an instance of the superiority of "uncivilised" Germans

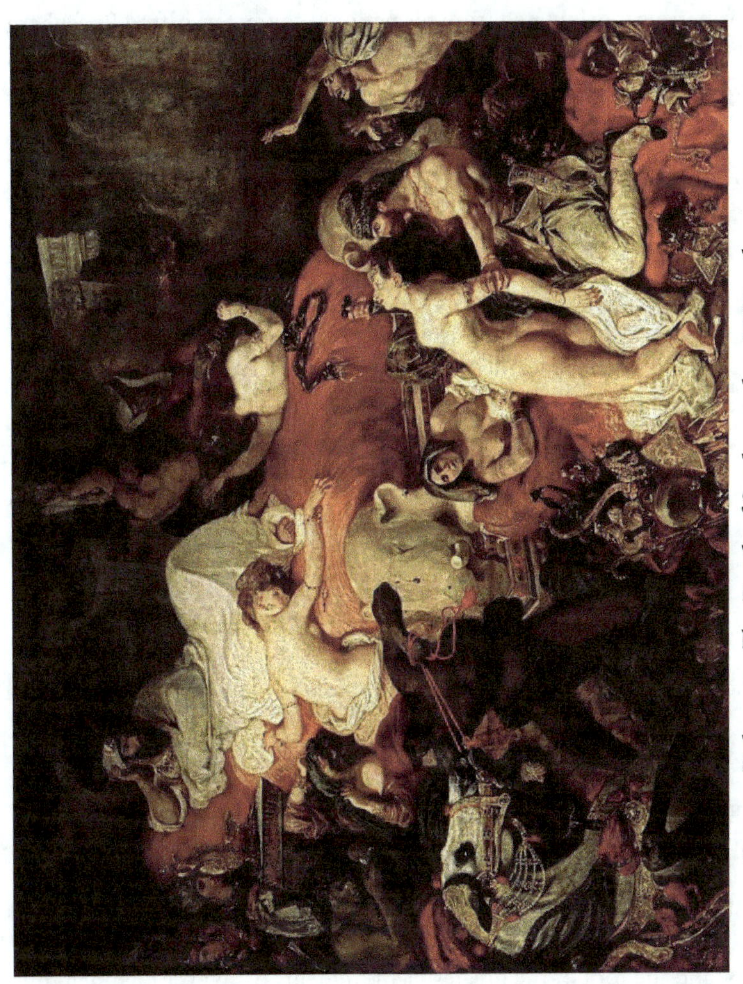

Eugene Delacroix, *The Death of Sardanapalus*, 1827, oil on canvas

over "civilised" Latins.[1] The Battle of Teutoburg was a patriotic subject for the Nazis, in search of new non-religious communal celebrations. Such sentiments underpinned the policy of *Naturschutz* (German: nature protection), championed by Walther Darré, which would conserve the remnants of wilderness and even re-introduce wild animals hunted to extinction.[2] For the Nazis, archaeology was a natural activity for the German, as it originated from his national character. Alfred Rosenberg (1893–1946), a trained architect and leading ideologist of Nazi cultural policy, wrote that Germans were driven by innate curiosity.

> Germanic man appeared in world history as creator. He sailed around the entire earth. He discovered millions of worlds. In the heat of a tropical sun he excavated prehistoric, long forgotten cities. He researched poems and myths. He sought after legendary fortresses. With indescribable effort he deciphered papyrus rolls, hieroglyphics and inscriptions on clay fragments. He investigated thousand year old mortar and stone. He learned all the languages of the world. He lived among Bushmen, Indians, Chinese, and formed for himself a varied picture of the souls of the peoples. He saw technology, morals, art and religion grow up from beginnings of the most diverse kinds of works of a different nature. He comprehended personality because he was himself one. He grasped the activity of peoples as action, as shaped spiritual power, as an expression of a uniquely personal inwardness. He not only had interest in the fact that men thought and acted in such and such a way, but he did not rest until he had learned to grasp the inner forces—whether rational or intuitive—which shaped the destiny of civilisations.[3]

Archaeology would be a field prioritised by Nazi—and other nationalist regimes—as it potentially offered proof of assertions about the cultural achievements and territorial possession advanced to justify political claims. Scientific analysis of archaeological finds could turn Romantic notions into indisputable fact.[4] In the case of Nazi-endorsed historical research, one aim was to prove that the Germans were pure-blood Aryans, and the root of the greatest achievements of civilisation, including those of classical Greek culture. Efforts included a 1938 expedition to Tibet to uncover assumed links between ancient Tibetans and Aryans and modern Germans, including anthropometric scrutiny of bones. There were efforts to confirm the migration theories of the German archaeologist and philologist Gustaf Kossinna (1858–1931) regarding Germanic tribes as descendants of Aryan migration. These projects were overseen by Amt Rosenberg, a group headed by Rosenberg.

The search for pre-Christendom bonds of kinship—both at home and abroad—became inextricably bound up with the political aim of establishing new communal ties and national foundational myths within Western states unmoored from previously accepted authority. Nationalism, race, and art had been tied together, as we find with regard to Romanticism in northern countries.

# ENDNOTES

All online references retrieved August-September 2022.

1    See Schama, 2004, pp. 88–100.

2    Schama, 2004, p. 82. "Arguably, no German government had ever taken the protection of the German forests more seriously than the Third Reich and its Reichsforstminister Göring." Schama, 2004, p. 119.

3    Rosenberg, 1937, unpag.

4    Schama, 2004, p. 79

# ART AND
# NATIONAL CHARACTER

It was at the founding of modern art history—at its conception, one could say—that the character of a landscape and the habits and customs of its people were considered to be the core of its school of art. The French diplomat and art critic Abbé Jean-Baptiste Dubos (1670–1742) wrote a discourse on poetry and painting entitled *Critical Reflections on Poetry and Painting* (1719), in which he attributed different national characters to distinctive air of particular regions. Later thinkers would reject the concept of air as a transmitter of distinctive characteristics, instead attributing to climate, food and geography such influence.

In his 1755 essay "On the Imitation of Greek Works in Painting and Sculpture", which established him as an authority, the German classics scholar and art critic Johann Joachim Winckelmann (1717–1768) set out the case that beauty derives from the correct imitation of beautiful subjects:

> The imitation of beauty is either reduced to a single object, and is *individual*, or, gathering observations from single ones, *composes of these one whole*. The former we call copying, drawing a portrait; 'tis the straight way to Dutch forms and figures; whereas the other leads to general beauty, and its ideal images, and is the way the Greeks took.[1]

Greek art developed to such a high level because the environment developed bodies of great beauty ("The forms of the Greeks, prepared to beauty, by the influence of the mildest and purest sky, became perfectly elegant by their early exercises."[2]), the social conditions of the day led to artists becoming familiar with the nude form in all activities, and the thought and character of the Greeks were ennobled by familiarity with beauty and accomplishments of the greatest standard.

Winckelmann's advice for modern artists was:

> There is but one way for the moderns to become great, and perhaps unequalled; I mean, by imitating the antients. [...] The ideas of unity and perfection, which he acquired in meditating on antiquity, will help him to combine, and to ennoble the more scattered and weaker beauties of our [current day] Nature. Thus he will improve every beauty he discovers in it, and by comparing the beauties of nature with the ideal, form rules for himself.[3]

Points that a modern artist should imitate from the ancients are contour, drapery, and expression, as well as following the Greek's workmanship in sculpture, painting, and allegory.

For Winckelmann, place, society, biology, culture, and thought were intimately interconnected in a set of causal relations. No element stood in isolation. The elements grew together, reinforcing one another, gradually over the course of centuries. Art arose from that nexus. The only way of producing art that came close to the perfection of ancient Greece would be by a nation submitting to its own nature—shared values arising from kinship—and allowing that to be expressed according to the place—environment. It would, perforce, be different, as peoples are different, but it would only reach its full potential through observing what seem to be a universal constant of great creators being true to the character of their own people located in their specific homeland.

We find such ideas commonly in discourses on the character of individuals from specific places. Some of these characteristics (or stereotypes) derive from accurate observations, although they do not apply to all individuals of that group. The inhabitant of a hot region is naturally languid, conserving energy in heat of the day. The inhabitant of a fertile region is lazy because he does not have to work hard for sustenance, because it is provided for him by nature. The inhabitant of a mountainous region is resilient because he subjected to hardship and is self-reliant because he spends most of his life isolated from the people and materials common in the lowlands. This character is found in the architecture, which is also produced using local materials and built to respond to local conditions. This confluence of local character, conditions and materials makes architecture the ultimate indicator of a place and its people. The expansion of international architecture, with its common building materials, techniques, and styles, in the globalist era is a deracinating phenomenon precisely because it erases historical difference and forestalls localist solutions. Joseph Friedrich zu Racknitz (1744–1818) wrote his treatise on the architecture of different nations (published 1796–9) that described the architecture and decoration of different lands as indicative of environment and national character.[4] Many of his observations extend the conclusions that Winckelmann drew from ancient Greek art.

Before German unification, French woman of letters Madame de Staël (1766–1817) made observations on national character and the Germans. "National character influences literature, literature and philosophy influence religion, and the whole can make fully known each part." A subscriber to Romantic conceptions of nationalism, Madame de Staël offered a superficial description of the Germans which seems more platitudinous than rigorous:

> The resemblance among the Teutonic nations in unmistakable. Independence and loyalty always distinguished these nations; they have always been good and faithful, and it is perhaps for that very reason that their writings bear the mark of melancholy. For it often happens that nations, as individuals, suffer for their virtues.[5]

Romanticism became a focal point for German nationalists in the Napoleonic era. The belief in the naturalness and necessity of a unified German state for the people of the German lands became a cause described as "Pan-Germanism". This was the impetus for the search for a mental outlook and culture to bind together German-speaking peoples in adjacent lands, including those who spoke dialects of German. The *Völkisch* conception of blood kinship was invoked by nationalists to overcome differences in tradition, culture, dialect, and religion across lands that had never been united previously. To form a single German state, commonalities had to be stressed, and an appeal to eternal constants made. This could be done through Romanticism, with its emphasis on the links of modern man to prehistory, engagement with pre-Christian and pagan beliefs, a renewed focus on the symbiotic relationship between man and the landscape and a tendency towards nativism (as opposed to the Renaissance and classicist emphasis on Hellenism). Thus, Romanticism became the favoured intellectual and artistic framework for cultural nationalists in the 1790–1850 period in Europe.

Scandinavian Romantic nationalism has been described as starting in the summer of 1802, when Danish-Norwegian geologist and natural philosopher Henrich Steffens (1773–1845) delivered a lecture in

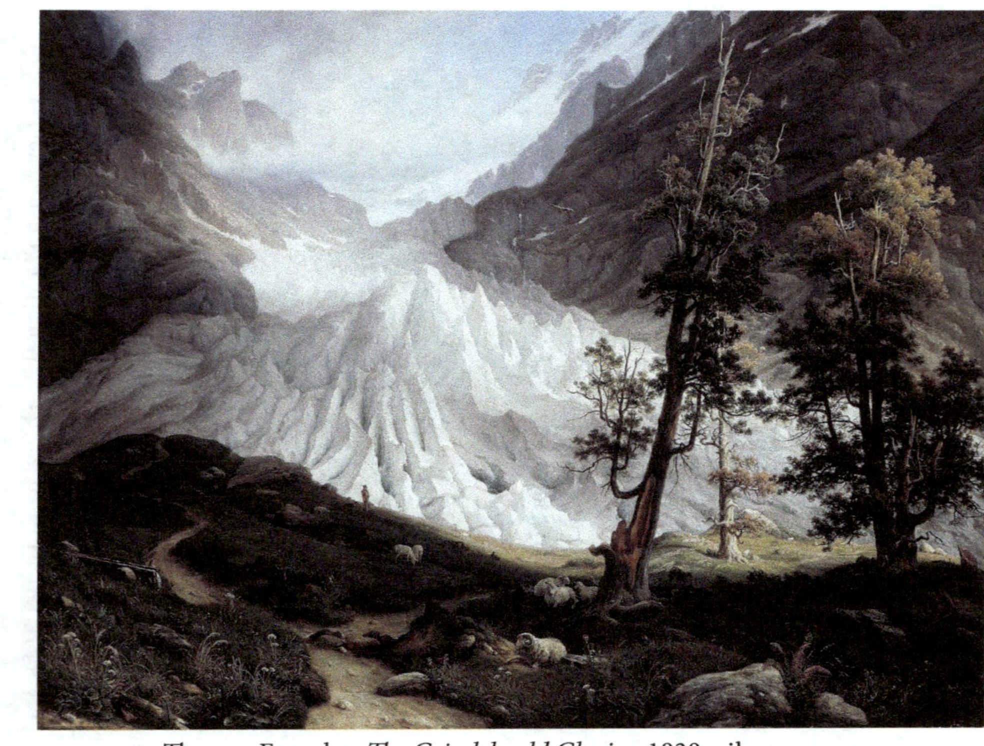

Thomas Fearnley, *The Grindelwald Glacier*, 1838, oil on canvas

Copenhagen. Influenced by his teacher at Jena University, German Romantic Friedrich Schelling (1775–1854) and his scientific studies, Steffens transmitted to leading Scandinavian intellectuals ideas about the influence of landscape on national character.[6] The contemporaneous ideas of the beautiful and sublime were particularly applicable to the wilder coastal scenes of Norway. This discussion would be deepened in the period of national reassessment following Denmark's loss of Norway to Sweden in 1814 (as the result of the Treaty of Kiel), causing Danes to seek to understand themselves in relation to their homeland, partly through landscape painting of Denmark, specifically after the loss of Norway. At the end of the century, Finns would acclaim Akseli Gallén-Kallela (1865–1931) as their national painter following his production of Symbolist paintings of their national myth, the *Kalevala*.

Politically progressive Russian artists judged that the formation of a national art would allow the character of the people to emerge through art, free from direction and censorship of the Czar and the Church. Nationalism would be a revolutionary force, unharnessing the potential of the people (with their folkcraft) and the intellectuals (with their fine art). Ivan Nikolayevich Kramskoy (1837–1887) wrote an article in 1877 that was forceful and absolute:

> The principal thesis I should like to put forward, and of which one can never say enough, is as follows: art can only be national, it must be national and nothing else but national. The idea, thus expressed, is perhaps shared by many, but practice differs from theory to a great extent. One need not concern oneself with being national in art, all one needs is to be allowed to create in complete freedom. With full artistic freedom, nationality, as a spontaneous force, will naturally (like water down a slope) impregnate everything created by artists of a given nation, even those artists who, due to their personal inclinations, distance themselves from the influence of traditional folklore.[7]

Across Europe in the nineteenth century—and in the Americas slightly later—we see national schools developing in new nation states, distinguishing national characteristics, and adapted to local issues. The Hudson River School and the Tonalist movement in the USA are mildly nationalist descendants of Romanticism, whereas in the 1920s the Regionalist movement (more artistically and chronologically distant from Romanticism) blended realism and Modernism. At the same time as the American Regionalists were working, in Mexico the Muralists developed a patriotic social realism, incorporating references to native folkcraft, responding to the political conditions and the stylistic idioms of the 1920s. Romanticism is not the automatic choice for nationalist expression, but it lends itself to such a cause.

Before we look more at the role played by Romanticism in German nation-founding, we should examine another nationalist movement within German lands that occurred in the same era: the Jewish Zionist project.

# ENDNOTES


1    Winckelmann, 1765, ch. 1.

2    Winckelmann, 1765, ch. 1.

3    Winckelmann, 1765, ch. 1.

4    Joseph Friedrich zu Racknitz, Simon Swynfen Jervis (*ed./trans.*), *A Rare Treatise on Interior Decoration and Architecture. Joseph Friedrich zu Racknitz's Presentation and History of the Taste of the Leading Nations*, Getty Publications, Los Angeles, 2020 (1796–9). For my review, see https://alexanderadamsart. wordpress.com/2020/06/16/racknitz-architectural-taste-and-orientalism/.

5    Madame de Staël, 1964, p. 218.

6    Stougaard-Nielsen, 2020, p. 168.

7    Kramskoy, in Harrison, 1998, p. 523.

# ROMANTICISM AND JEWISH ZIONISM

The aspiration for a Jewish state originated in the egalitarian idealism of the French Revolution.[1] The modern political Zionist movement was founded in 1896 by Jewish Austrian author Theodor Herzl (1860–1904). The aim of the movement was to establish a political and geographical state that would be a homeland for the Jewish diaspora, preferably in the territory of the Holy Land. Given the fractured history of the Jews, any such project would be internally controversial and rejected by some. The foundation of a state is attended by questions about the legitimacy of that state. One test of legitimacy of a nation is the maintenance of a continuous and distinctive cultural tradition in respect to the arts. No unique visual-art form or style (with the exception of calligraphy and religious regalia) had been developed by diaspora Jews—a problem for a Zionist state which sought to present itself as more than an artificial political construction made for the advantage of an ethno-religious group. In short, every nation needs a range of symbols and visual archetypes which will be incorporated into its civic life and the consciousness of its members.[2]

In light of such debates, Jewish artist Ephraim Moses Lilien (1874–1925) carefully considered the necessity for a Jewish art, made by and for Jews. Lilien was born in the Austro-Hungarian Empire, visited Palestine, and lived and worked in Germany. He drew pictures of Jewish stories for reproduction as journal and book illustrations, primarily made around 1900 to 1914 and published in Germany. In his art, paradigmatic images of manly Jewish men (often modelled on the imposing appearance of Herzl[3]) and beautiful Jewish women were intended to form a shared bond of culture necessary for nationhood, as well as dispel negative widely circulated stereotypes of Jews (the hook-nosed merchant, the bookish urbanite, the overbearing mother). Lilien illustrated poems about Jews written by Börries, Freiherr von Münchhausen (1874–1945):

> In contrast to the common image of the Jew as shabby, timorous, beaten down, subsisting on mean or ignominious trades, and covered in heavy dark clothing emblematic of his alienation from the natural world, including his own body, Münc[h]hausen's poems, inspired perhaps by certain texts of Nietzsche, celebrated the epic-heroic qualities of the ancient Hebrews, their courage, strength, and natural beauty.[4]

Lilien wanted his art to contribute to the secondary aim of Zionism (as set out by Martin Buber), that of raising Jewish self-esteem. Lilien's style was in the form of small illustrations, monochromatic, graphic in character and influenced by Romanticism, Symbolism, Jugendstil, and Art Nouveau, incorporating Hebrew calligraphy. His art was not a style that arose organically from the racial and religious bonds of Judaism; it was, however, an artificial construction invoking a common heritage and appealing to Romantic idealisations, instated in place of a conspicuously absent shared Jewish visual-arts culture. The Biblical injunction against graven images and the dispersed dislocated nature of the Jewish people meant that such visual styles and pictorial languages could not develop; whether or not—had the injunction not existed—a Jewish art style would have developed due to national/ethnic character is a moot point.

Buber, as a leading Zionist and supporter of Lilien, admitted that Jewish art had deficits precisely because the people had no land. "Only when each people [*Volk*] expresses its own being," Buber had declared in 1900, "can it increase the common treasury." In that same spirit—reminiscent of Johann Gottfried Herder's early Romantic combination of historical particularism and Enlightenment universalism, but now invested with the nationalist fervour and the growing preoccupation with race of the late nineteenth century—Buber accepted that the revival of Jewish culture was "a tributary of the new Renaissance of Humanity [*ein Teilstrom der neuen Menschheitsrenaissance*]," and acknowledged that emancipation and enhanced contact with the surrounding world had been the conditions that produced not only "the wretched episode of assimilationism [*die armselige Episode 'Assimilation'*]" but also the current revival of artistic creativity among Jews. Nevertheless, he insisted, "the bare fact that we again have artists is [...] not enough to establish that there is a Jewish art." It was necessary to move beyond the

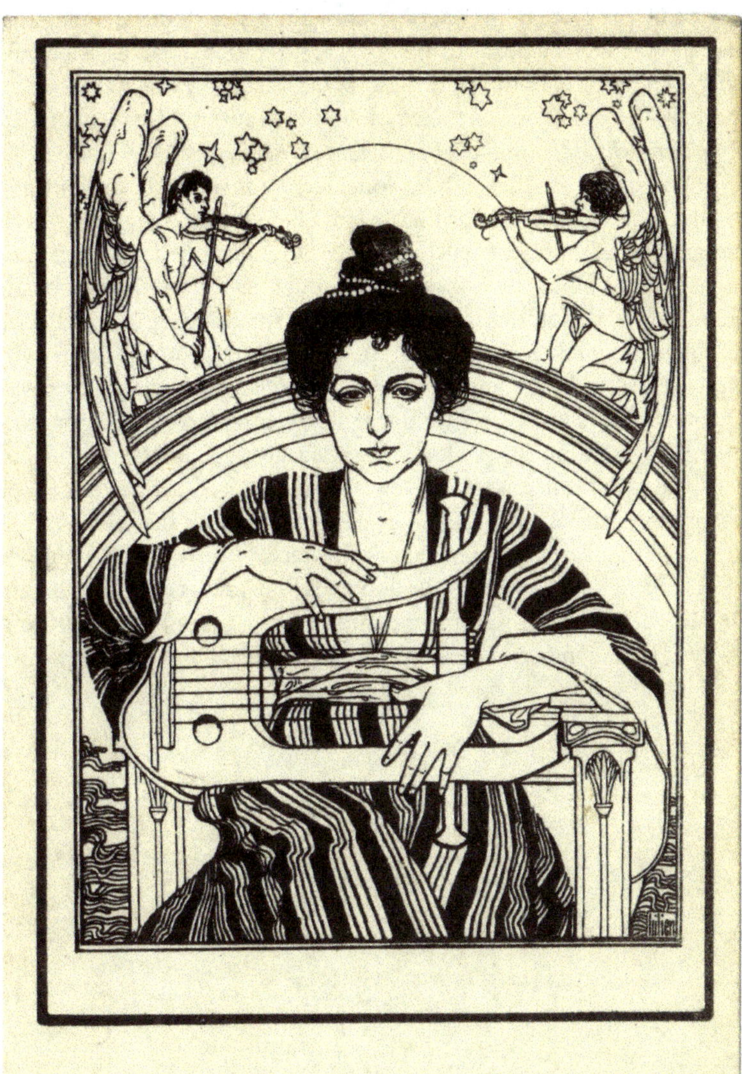



Moses Ephraim Lilien, *The Songs of Life*, 1910, illustration

mere existence of artists of Jewish origin. If that was finally beginning to happen, Buber claimed, it was because "one or another of our artists, moved by the force of his Jewish blood, put his ear to his people's soul and allowed it to shape his works." The regeneration of Jewish art would not be completed, however, until it had taken root in the native soil of the Jews, for "a national art needs a land to grow out of [*eine nationale Kunst braucht einen Erdboden, aus dem sie herauswächst*]."[5]

The example of Lilien can be considered a mark against the idea of artistic schools springing primarily from hereditable characteristics, as his art was assembled from borrowed styles and used newly minted archetypes. As Gossman observes, although some Jewish symbolism, characters and clothing is included in Lilien's drawings, the art itself is conventional Jugendstil—the Austrian form of international Art Nouveau. Many commentators observe that there is nothing Jewish *per se* about Lilien's art. Art critic Edgar Regener dissented, claiming that Lilien's form (if not his style) was Jewish. Regener wrote that Lilien's art "belonged in the essentially Jewish tradition of *Buchschmuck* (book decoration), the area of artistic expression to which the Jew is drawn 'by the particular national capacity of his race.'"[6] However one judges its visual character, Lilien's art is undoubtedly a prime example of Romantic nationalism, both sentimental and utilitarian in nature, albeit one evolved by a member of a group without a defined homeland.[7]

# ENDNOTES


1    Barnet Litvinoff, *Road to Jerusalem*, Weidenfeld & Nicolson, London, 1965, p. 15.

2    At this time, Jewish artists were only just emerging as leading figures, mainly in Modernist schools. Prior to 1900, Jews contributed disproportionately little to the visual fine arts. Apart from other narratives on this, Lombroso cites statistics of "celebrities" in various fields, Europeans having 40 per 100,000 and Jews 34, in the category "artists". Lombroso, 1917, p. 134.

3    "Max Nordau [called] for a *'Muskeljudentum'* [muscular Jewish people]." Gossman, 2004, p. 40.

4    Gossman, 2004, p. 33.

5    Gossman, 2004, pp. 42–3.

6    Gossman, 2004, p. 46.

7    See also Swarts, 2020.

# DE GOBINEAU ON
# CULTURE FROM RACE

The French aristocrat and statesman Joseph Arthur, Comte de Gobineau (1816–1882) wrote *The Moral and Intellectual Diversity of the Races* in the 1850s, refuting many of the assertions and assumptions of the French Revolution, most specifically notions of *liberté, égalité, fraternité* between men. H. Holtz, commentor on the first English-language edition summarises de Gobineau's case:

> The leading proposition in this volume is, that the civilization originated and developed by a race, is the clearest index of its character—the mirror in which its principal features are truthfully reflected. In other words, that every race, capable of developing a civilization, will develop one peculiar to itself, and impossible to every other.[1]

De Gobineau sees culture as formed and directed by the aristocracy, later debased and diluted by the bourgeois and merchants. The initial state, achieved once stability has been secured, is the foundation of institutions that benefit society. The purity of the race and the stability of the society maintain the correctness of institutions. The influence of other races introduces changes not intended to benefit the original institutions but to serve the interests of newcomers. Although some vitality may be derived thereby, overall, the trajectory is inevitably towards the degradation of institutions and society.

The author defines race and attributes biological and temperamental characteristics to them.[2] Societies are formed in the image of the race and to serve that race. Societies are therefore different, with some being superior. De Gobineau grades the Teutonic race as the highest. "Wherever our state of civilization extends, it is characterized by two traits; the first, that the population contains a greater or less admixture of Teutonic blood; the other, that it is Christian."[3] However, he argues that race is more important than politics, religion, or geography:

> Before concluding this picture, I would add that the immense superiority of the white races in all that regards the intellectual faculties, is joined to an inferiority as strikingly marked, in the intensity of sensations. Though his whole structure is more vigorous, the white man is less gifted in regard to the perfection of the senses than either the black or the yellow, and therefore less solicited and less absorbed by animal gratifications.[4]

He insists on the persistence of racial characteristics among groups subsequent to migration, which he claims as evidence of heredity as a key to transmission of values and interests. The book, which was widely translated and discussed in the second half of the nineteenth century, became a keystone for discussion on race and culture, pro and contra.

# ENDNOTES

1    H. Holtz in de Gobineau, 1856, pp. 234–5.

2    de Gobineau's classification of races was considered too speculative and potentially misleading by Holz, who omitted this passage from the 1856 edition. H. Holtz in de Gobineau, 1856, pp. 268–9.

3    de Gobineau, 1856, p. 280.

4    de Gobineau, 1856, p. 454.

# NORDIC CULTURE

Developing ideas set out by de Gobineau, Max Nordau (1843–1923) wrote in his book *Entartung* (*Degeneration*) (1892–3) in quasi-scientific terms about the link between temperament, nationality, and aesthetics.

> It is evident that a period which suffers from general organic fatigue must necessarily be a pessimistic period. We recognise also the constant habit which consciousness has of inventing, *post facto*, apparently plausible motives, borrowed from its store of representations, and in conformity with the rules of its formal logic, to justify the emotional states of which it has acquired the knowledge. Thus, for the datum of the pessimistic disposition of mind, which is the consequence of organic fatigue, there arises the pessimist philosophy as an ulterior creation of interpretative consciousness. In Germany, in conformity with the speculative tendency and high intellectual culture of the German people, this state of mind has sought expression in philosophical systems. In France it has adopted an artistic form in accordance with the predominating æsthetic character of the national mind. M. Emile Zola and his naturalism are the French equivalent of the German Schopenhauer and his philosophical pessimism. That naturalism should see nothing in the world but brutality, infamy, ugliness, and corruption, corresponds with all that we know of the laws of thought.[1]

Nordau goes on to say that Zola is influenced by his preoccupation with ordure, base sensations and the naturally unpleasant, because it is his nature. Whether naturalism in artistry is closely associated with temperamental coarseness—and how that might be associated with national character—Nordau leaves open to interpretation. (It is worth noting that at this time both the naturalism school and the Decadence move-ment—polar opposites—were considered deviants by traditionalists, both schools having rejected the conventions of the status quo of the late nineteenth century.) Nordau is not the last writer to infer that the climatically cold north imparted racial hygiene and generated culture as an antiseptic purgative. The notion of the bracing north imparting health (and the south acting as the antithesis) exerts a powerful imag-inative hold over those seeking to associate national temperament and social culture with geographical conditions. Nordau thought in terms of sickness rather than sin, but his conception of sickness has moral imputations. Consider the social revulsion and shame at the venereal disease syphilis, considered as illness and product of sin.

*Degeneration* was dedicated by Nordau to Cesare Lombroso (1835–1909), the Italian criminologist, whose work formed part of the wave of scientific investigation in the areas of sociology, psychology, psychi-atry, anthropology, and anthropometry which sought causes for social phenomena in the inherited characteristics of individuals and groups. It was this work that was taken up by supporters of scientific racism, which sometimes proved an ill fit with Romantic myths and the Nazi appeal to instinctive loyalty of blood and soil, as these new scientif-ic theories undermined long-standing assumptions. Although Nazis paraphrased Nordau's Social Darwinism, they mostly avoided outright citations: as well as being an ardent racist, Nordau was well known to be a Jew and a Zionist.

# ENDNOTES

1    Nordau, 1898, p. 498.

# NORWEGIAN RACE SCIENCE

In the nineteenth century, the ideas of "race science", anthropology (including anthropometry) and nationalism (including national self-determination and national character) were intertwined. The allied (though distinct) concepts of German, Norse, Nordic, Teutonic, and Aryan peoples demanded scientific classification in order for them to be instrumentalised by nationalists, politicians, administrators, and eugenicists for public policy, as well as by applied by historians, archaeologists, ethnographers, and other professionals in the human-science field.

Historians Gerhard Schøning (1722–1780), Rudolf Keyser (1803–1864) and Peter Andreas Munch (1810–1863) theorised about a North Germanic settlement of Norway, with Denmark and Sweden being settled by Southern German Goths. This Norwegian School of History would describe Norway as ethnically and culturally distinct from Denmark and Sweden. A theory that fortuitously separated Norway from the two neighbouring powers, which had had control over Norway for centuries, was a gift to nationalists, who could claim racial justification for independence from the two main powers of Scandinavia. Not that such theories did not receive opposition from distinguished Norwegian academics, including Ludvig Kristensen Daa.

While the Norwegian School of History was in decline in academia by the end of the century, it was revived by anthropometric scientists, who set out to record anatomies of various peoples, living and dead, and assign them to racial groups. Over the period of the 1880s to 1930s, Kristian Emil Schreiner, Alette Schreiner, Carl Oscar Eugen Arbo, Gustav Adolph Guldberg and Halfdan Bryn pursued data-gathering exercises on a small scale, while lobbying the Norwegian Academy of

Science and Letters, university departments, hospitals, the government and the military for funding and manpower in order to conduct extensive anthropometry on living Norwegians. This eventually led to the Norwegian Racial Survey of 1920–1. Although there were no specific plans for the use of the data, it was expected that race scientists would compare this database on the Norwegian people to historic skeletons, in order to determine changes, historical continuity, and migration patterns. In 1932, the husband of Alette Schreiner, co-director of the Racial Survey, pronounced on the evaluated Nordic man:

> [I]n the popular-scientific radio-lecture *The Races of Europe*, Kristian Emil Schreiner dismissed the idea of 'the Nordic man as the sole creator of the highest intellectual culture'. [...] The Nordic race was a 'race of warriors and explorers, hardy, enterprising, independent and adventurous men', but as creators of culture, they lacked persistence. With regard to such properties, 'the Mediterranean race and the Oriental races were clearly equivalent to the Nordic'.[1]

The Schreiners agreed that national characteristics existed, and could be racial in origin; also that cultures were specific to races, without claiming priority for their own Nordic people as supreme in the cultural field.

Denmark-Norway had a small body of research scientists and hence a very limited pool of race scientists. The fact that Norwegian anthropology was such a small field—with most colleagues being overseas and research literature not being in Dano-Norwegian—meant that Norwegians were influenced by foreign scientists, many of them German.[2] At this time, German scientists went to Africa and territories in part of the short-lived German colonial empire in order to conduct measuring of native peoples for comparative purposes. Scientists were trained by technicians in the skills and materials needed for plaster-cast making. Casts of the bodies and faces of natives were brought back to Germany and distributed to university anthropology departments across the country. Casts and moulds remain in the Berliner Gipsformerei (German: Berlin plaster workshop) to this day, deemed too politically contentious to be exhibited or published.[3]

# ENDNOTES

1    Kyllingstad, 2014, ch. 8.

2    "Anthropologists in Western Europe operated on the international stage: they were connected with each other through personal and professional networks [...] The actual research, however, was usually carried out within a national context, was often financed by national funding bodies and conducted by national research institutions, and had the principal aim of studying the racial composition and history of the national or colonial population. [...] Hence the discipline's development in one country was related, but not necessarily identical, to its development in other national contexts. [...] In the case of Norway, the rise and eventual fall of the concept of the Nordic master race was affected but not determined by shifts in its status within the international scientific world." Kyllingstad, 2014, introduction.

3    See Veronika Tocha, *et al.*, *Near Life: The Gipsformerei. 200 Years of Casting Plaster*, Prestel, Munich, 2020.

# MUNCH AND THE NORWEGIAN NATIONAL CHARACTER

Edvard Munch may have concurred with Lombroso's 1888 book *L'uomo di genio* (*The Man of Genius*), in which Lombroso explained the way heritability and race correlate to madness and genius. Back in 1888, Lombroso had noted the large number of geniuses who were Jewish, then drew a corelation between genius, neurosis, and madness. "Insanity. — It is curious to note that the Jewish elements in the population furnish four and even six times as many lunatics as the rest of the population."[1] Lombroso is clear that genius (and madness) is born (and inherited) rather than made. "The influence of race is as visible in genius as in insanity. Education counts for little, heredity for much."[2] (He comments that geniuses are rarely women.[3]) Munch considered himself on the edge of madness most of his life; he thought that his sensitivity and disposition left him more open to insights of genius and fancies of madness. In 1908 he was hospitalised due to a mental collapse and required months of treatment to recover.

Munch thought that what destined him to be an artist also threatened his health and sanity; he dwelt on hereditary traits and weaknesses. His mother and sister died of tuberculosis; another sister was confined to a mental asylum for a time and gradually lost her hold on reality before she reached middle age; his father was "temperamentally nervous and obsessively religious—to the point of psychoneurosis. From him I inherited the seeds of madness. The angels of fear, sorrow and death stood by my side since the day I was born."[4] The painter was touched by both tuberculosis and madness and survived both. Marked by the impact of the inheritance of family, people, land, and culture, Munch's art is both deeply personal and very Norwegian.

On the subject of national character in relation to Munch, we can turn to a passage written by a Norwegian author, who described the residents of Skien, a small town in Norway. It may serve as Norwegian-character sketch by a Norwegian:

> They appear sanguine but are often melancholic. They analyse and pass judgement on themselves… proud and stiff, combative when anyone threatens their interest; they dislike being told. They are reserved and cautious towards strangers, do not easily accept their friendship, and are not very forthcoming even to their own kin… afraid openly to surrender to a mood or to let themselves be carried away; they suffer from shyness of the soul.[5]

Another author described Norwegians:

> Dour, intelligent and highly argumentative, he holds fast to his own opinion as he holds to his few acres of land. His virtue is tenacity, his vice obstinacy. He is not interested in the arts, though given to strong views on law or theology. […] In a country where the majority are self-employed as farmers or sailors, the main characteristic is independence—a firm and sometimes fierce self-sufficiency that encourages sardonic freedom of speech. The Norwegian abroad, or among strangers, is strong and silent: at home he is more likely merely to be strong.[6]

The author goes on to describe the Norwegian beyond social circumstances and in environmental ones:

> The Norwegian may appear stolid and hard-headed, but in moments of excitement the stolidity disappears. The strength of Norway is shown negatively, in endurance and control, in unshakable and ponderous consistency, qualities bred of life in a hard land; but it is steel which strikes a spark out of flint; and as an explosion is violent in proportion to the pressure released, sudden flashes of recklessness, blind to risk and deaf to good council, will leap out, instantaneous and shattering.[7]

The author then goes on to describe the playwriting of Henrik Ibsen (1828–1906) as derived from this national character which springs from environment:

Ibsen's plays are built on this national rhythm, the fundamental rhythm of the Norwegian character. Each depends
on a culmination of slow pressure and ends in an explosion.[8]

His writing can be understood only in terms of the Norse,
with its clear, pungent but concrete vocabulary, its strong,
live metaphors ('we felt our hearts *beat strongly towards
him*') its lack of reverberation or overtones. It is clear and
fine as mountain air.[9]

We can say that the Nordic temperament is popularly considered to be
meditative, withdrawn, pensive, and undemonstrative. Why might that
be? In Scandinavia and Russia, the geography of long sunlit summer
nights lead to prolonged contemplation of nature, bearing in mind the
isolation and loneliness of the extended winter nights both past and
ahead. The north (outside of cities) is sparsely populated; people are
isolated from each other and the rest of the world (traditionally) and
must be self-reliant and sensitive to nature, which can be dangerous
and unforgiving. Confronting the implacable harshness of nature leads
men to understand the insignificance of individual man. This leads to
a contemplative nature prone to melancholy and brooding but with a
strong strain of practicality, determination, stamina, and fortitude.[10]
We could say that isolation and suspicion of outsiders characterises the
rural Nordic person. Whether one sees that as a negative trait depends
on where one lies on the xenophilia/xenophobia axis. It is often said
that Russians and Scandinavians are heavy drinkers, compensating for
innate reticence and social isolation and the long periods of enforced
inactivity, caused due to hostile weather and darkness.[11]

To the harsh climate, we can add the effect of poverty, malnutrition,
and tuberculosis over most of Norway in the pre-twentieth century era.
Fear, loss, grief, and the resilience to overcome them shaped the character of Norwegian life at this time, and this necessarily conditioned
the society and its material culture. Munch may not have had the
severe poverty that Ibsen and Knut Hamsun (1859–1952) (discussed
later) experienced in their childhoods, but he lost family members to
tuberculosis. All three of them left Norway to earn money, broaden
their cultural horizons, hone their crafts, and reach wider audiences.
They had ambivalent relationships with their homeland, wrestling with
disappointment when their achievements were not acclaimed as they
hoped that they would be. Being abroad sharpened their sense of their
Norwegian identity.[12] Not least, all three Norwegians lived through a
period when Norway reached a state of independence, which required
a reassessment of what it meant to be Norwegian, as opposed to being

Danish or Swedish, which was done in part by looking to the literature of the past and making new Norwegian culture. This process involved detaching the different dialects of Norwegian from the standard civic language of Dano-Norwegian.[13] This process of differentiation and national reappraisal the Norwegians had in common with the Germans.[14]

# ENDNOTES


1	Lombroso, 1917, p. 136.

2	Lombroso, 1917, p. 137.

3	It should be noted that Lombroso is unreliable in many areas, not least because some of his information seems incomplete or erroneous.

4	Munch, quoted in Prideaux, 2005, p. 2.

5	Oskar Mosfjeld, *Henrik Ibsen og Skien*, Gyldendal, Oslo, 1949, p. 57, quoted in Prideaux, 2005, p. 2.

6	Bradbrook, 1966, p. 18.

7	Bradbrook, 1966, pp. 18–9.

8	Bradbrook, 1966, p. 19.

9	Bradbrook, 1966, p. 24.

10	This has also been attributed to Seasonal Affective Disorder, in which deprivation of sunlight and vitamin D causes increased depression.

11	Statistical data is split on this. One source suggests that higher latitudes are correlated with higher alcohol consumption: https://www.alcoholproblemsandsolutions.org/geography-of-alcohol-and-drinking/.  Another source gives data showing that consumption per head is only moderate in Scandinavia and slightly higher in Russia, while at its highest at lower latitude Western Europe: https://ourworldindata.org/alcohol-consumption. Lynn (op. cit, p. 7) has figures of Norway being a low-alcohol consumption and in alcoholism and liver cirrhosis, compared to France, with high consumption, alcoholism and cirrhosis.

12	Hamsun, 1947: "During my rather long life, in all the countries where I have travelled, and among the ethnic groups I have mingled with, I have ever and always preserved and upheld the homeland in my mind." Quoted in Sjølyst-Jackson, 2010, p. 8.

13	Hamsun revised the spelling of his earlier published writings to make them more Norwegian in the late 1900s, after Norwegian independence of 1905 and the first Norwegian language reform of 1907.

14	See Kyllingstad, 2014, ch. 4.

# FROM FICHTE
# TO PAN-GERMANISM

The German philosopher Johann Fichte's *Addresses to the German Nation* (1807–8) set out the unique qualities of the German people, including attachment to homeland and crafting the German language, which combine to create the German genius.

> So we may say that genius in foreign lands will strew with flowers the well-trodden military roads of antiquity, and weave a becoming robe for that wisdom of life which it will easily take for philosophy. The German spirit, on the other hand, will open up new shafts and bring the light of day into their abysses, and hurl up rocky masses of thoughts, out of which ages to come will build their dwellings. The foreign genius will be a delightful sylph, which hovers in graceful flight above the flowers that have sprung of themselves from its soil, settles on them without causing them to bend, and drinks up their refreshing dew. Or we may call it a bee, which with busy art gathers the honey from the same flowers and deposits it with charming tidiness in cells of regular construction. But the German spirit is an eagle, whose mighty body thrusts itself on high and soars on strong and well-practised wing into the empyrean, that it may rise nearer to the sun whereon it delights to gaze.[1]
>
> First of all and before all things: man does not form his scientific view in a particular way voluntarily and arbitrarily, but it is formed for him by his life, and is in reality the inner, and to him unknown, root of his own life, which has become his way of looking at things. It is what you really are in your inmost soul that stands forth to your outward eye, and you

would never be able to see anything else. If you are to see differently, you must first of all become different. Now, the inner essence of non-German ways, or of non-originality, is the belief in something that is final, fixed, and settled beyond the possibility of change, the belief in a border-line, on the hither side of which free life may disport itself, but which it is never able to break through and dissolve by its own power, and which it can never make part of itself. This impenetrable border-line is, therefore, inevitably present to the eyes of foreigners at some place or other, and it is impossible for them to think or believe except with such a border-line as a presupposition, unless their whole nature is to be transformed and their heart torn out of their body. They inevitably believe in death as Alpha and Omega, the ultimate source of all things and, therefore, of life itself.[2]

Seeking to raise national consciousness, Fichte called for educational reform and renewed trust in Germanic traditions and rejection of foreign influence. He did not define the German race *per se*, assuming it to be self-evidently obvious. The idea of German institutions intended to sustain and renew Germanness was specific to a period when Germany was divided into divided and competitive statelets. Fichte was considered a precursor of the Pan-Germanist movement that developed over the nineteenth century, and which was seen by many as an incomplete mission, following the 1871 unification of Germany under Bismarck, which failed to include all the lands occupied by Germans. The division of German-speaking peoples in states within the territories of Germany, Austria, Lichtenstein, the Netherlands, Belgium, France, Switzerland, Italy, Denmark, Poland, Bohemia (Czechoslovakia) and non-contiguous regions in Romania, Hungary, Russia and other lands, provided obstacles to national unification of German peoples. Germans in the Tyrol have more in common (historically, legally, commercially, and temperamentally) with neighbouring Italians than with German-speaking Friesians and Pomeranians. How could German nationalists unify one nation from an assembly of German peoples: Catholics and Protestants, speakers of Hochdeutsch, Plattdeutsch, Bavarian, Frisian, Swiss and other dialects, from lands geographically widespread? The regions had very different customs and histories. This generated diversity that was celebrated for its cultural richness, but which was detrimental to unification. "This division of Germany, fatal to her political influence, was nevertheless very favourable to all efforts to talent and the imagination."[3] History before 1871 was more likely to divide Germans than unite them. "There cannot be much love of country in a realm divided for several centuries, where Germans fought Germans almost always through foreign instigation."[4] In 1891, the Alldeutscher Verband (German: Pan-German League) was formed to further the cause.

Guy Tourlamain identifies the anti-urbanisation, pro-nationalist *Heimatkunstbewegung* [German: homeland art movement] as a forerunner to later developments:

> A largely middle class phenomenon, the *Heimatkunstbewegung* was at once an assertion of local patriotism and an expression of nationalist sentiment. It was a conscious celebration of regional differences within the national whole; 'Germanness' was embedded in the history and customs of Germany's many regions, whence it derived its strength. [Supporters of] the *Heimat* movement were not necessarily engaging in a political or social discourse, but at most in a community-building exercise. The *Heimatkunstbewegung*, however, took the sentiments of regional romanticism and used them as the basis for a nationalist discourse based on the relationship of the *Volk* with its native landscape. This idea later influenced a number of leading Nazis, most notably Walt[h]er Darré.[5]

*Heimatkunstbewegung* was intended to increase regional pride and closer identification between populations and their regions, but it also served to strengthen associations between not only people, land, and art but a wider German national consciousness.

Language, given German regional variations, divided as much as it united. Language also muddied the issue, since many peoples used German as a *lingua franca* without being German. This was one cause of animus from Pan-Germanists towards the multi-ethnic Austro-Hungarian Empire. The empire's hybrid nature and the willingness (the necessity even) of its rulers to offer parity between peoples within a German-speaking compact was the antithesis of ethno-nationalism. Unity through language was a route towards civic nationalism. Civic nationalism, as found in Austro-Hungary, presented a multi-cultural, multi-ethnic, inclusive, adopted, artificial nationhood articulated through democratic representation in a constitutional monarchy, equality, modernity, even a form of limited internationalism. Worse still (for Pan-Germanists), civic nationalism allowed for the absorption of immigrants and foreign influence, further diluting the Germanic population and culture. For pan-Germanists, the effort was not only to set up organisations and a nation that would serve the German people; it was to describe the German and separate him from the German-speaking non-German Czech, Swiss, Hungarian, Galician and Jew—if the Jew were to be classed as non-German. Hence the imperative for Pan-Germanists to reject language and the national status of individuals—and place of residence—as the defining characteristics of being German.[6] Instead, Pan-Germanists invoked specifics of national character alongside foundational ancestral associations of blood and kinship, arguing that a shared trunk to the tree of the German people connected the currently separated branches, while also using shifting parameters to exclude German-speaking non-Germans from the fraternity of Germans.[7]

Hitler admitted to problems with defining the German race, and traced political problems to a lack of homogeneity.

> Unfortunately the German national being is not based on a uniform racial type. The process of welding the original elements together has not gone so far as to warrant us in saying that a new race has emerged. On the contrary, the poison which has invaded the national body, especially since the Thirty Years' War, has destroyed the uniform constitution not only of our blood but also of our national soul. The open frontiers of our native country, the association with non-German foreign elements in the territories that lie all along those frontiers, and especially the strong influx of foreign blood into the interior of the Reich itself, has prevented any complete assimilation of those various elements, because the influx has continued steadily. Out of this melting-pot no new race arose. The heterogeneous elements continue to exist side by side. And the result is that, especially in times of crisis, when the herd usually flocks together, the Germans disperse in all directions.[8]

Pan-Germanist responses towards ideas of Nordic, Teutonic and Aryan racial types are complex. It is worth presenting one here, as it relates directly to Nazi attitudes towards Norwegians.

> Hans Friedrich Günther, a German nationalist and right-wing ideologue who wrote popular books on racial theory for the general public. Günther, who married a Norwegian woman and lived for a time in Norway, exalted the Norwegians. He believed that they had preserved the genetic superiority and nobility of the Nordic race because of their

geographical isolation from the Continent and through their ongoing connection with rural culture. In his best-selling 1922 book *Rassenkunde des deutschen Volkes* (Racial Studies of the German People), Günther ascribed to the Nordic man a sense of adventurousness, truthfulness, and justice; a strong feeling for landscape; a heroic and creative temperament; iron willpower and good judgment; and, importantly, an exceptional ability to conquer and lead.[9]

It was in the light of such heroizing ideals, combined with condemnation of the weakening effect of decades of military neutrality, that Nazi attitudes towards Norwegians should be understood.

## ENDNOTES

1    Johann Fichte, *Addresses to the German Nation*, 1807–8, Fifth Address.

2    Fichte, op. cit., Seventh Address.

3    Madame de Staël, 1964, p. 220.

4    Madame de Staël, 1964, p. 223.

5    Tourlamain, 2014, p. 36.

6    "Not every book written in German is a German book: not every writer writing in German is a German writer." Adolf Bartels, German journalist, opposing erection of a monument to Heinrich Heine in 1906. Quoted in Tourlamain, 2014, pp. 55–6.

7    We should be careful not to see the Nazis as simply a reiteration of Pan-Germanism. National Socialist ideology differed in significant respects from Pan-Germanism in its *Lebensraum* expansionist policy (although some Pan-Germanists were pro-colonisation), its technocratic managerialism, embrace of industrialisation, materialism and other aspects. National Socialism was explicitly anti-Semitic whereas Pan-Germanism could (and did) include anti-Semitic rhetoric, Pan-Germanists were sometimes indifferent to the "Jewish Question".

8    Hitler, *Mein Kampf*, 1925–6, p. 214, https://archive.org/details/Hitler_Adolf_-_Mein_Kampf/.

9    Stratigakos, 2022, p. 14.

# KNUT HAMSUN, NORDIC MAN AND NAZISM

Knut Hamsun's novel *Hunger* caused a sensation when it was published in 1890. The novel follows an impoverished journalist who wanders Christiania, destitute, starving, and homeless. He pawns clothes in order to eat and submits articles to journal editors, dreaming of not just sustenance but fame. It was based on the author's own experiences. In *Hunger*, the protagonist is driven almost mad with hunger. He becomes reckless and impetuous; scorning financial prudence and social caution, he dares fate to spite him. His mood swings conflict with his best interests and alienate him from others. His selfishness, roughness and wildness match the persistent indifference of so-called respectable bourgeois society towards one of their own, thereby exposing the insulation of the bourgeois Norwegian from the essential human struggles.

Later novels and stories by Hamsun presented Norwegian protagonists who reject urban *anomie*, base materialism, foreign customs, and modern standards of social acceptance. The stories set in Norway's coastal villages present an alternative to the deracinated life of the city in an age-old life rooted in the eternal season cycle, at the mercy of nature. Early critic Josef Wiehr wrote in 1922 that,

> The simple life of the man who works the land he regards as the most natural, most useful, and, therefore, the best. It must not be inferred that Hamsun is a utilitarian. But the man on the land leads the sanest and most healthful life and produces what he needs to sustain it, enjoying therefore a larger degree of independence than the rest. Inasmuch as the modern development draws people farther and farther away from rural life, it is most harmful, and the culture it is supposed to produce is but a sham; through it the race simply

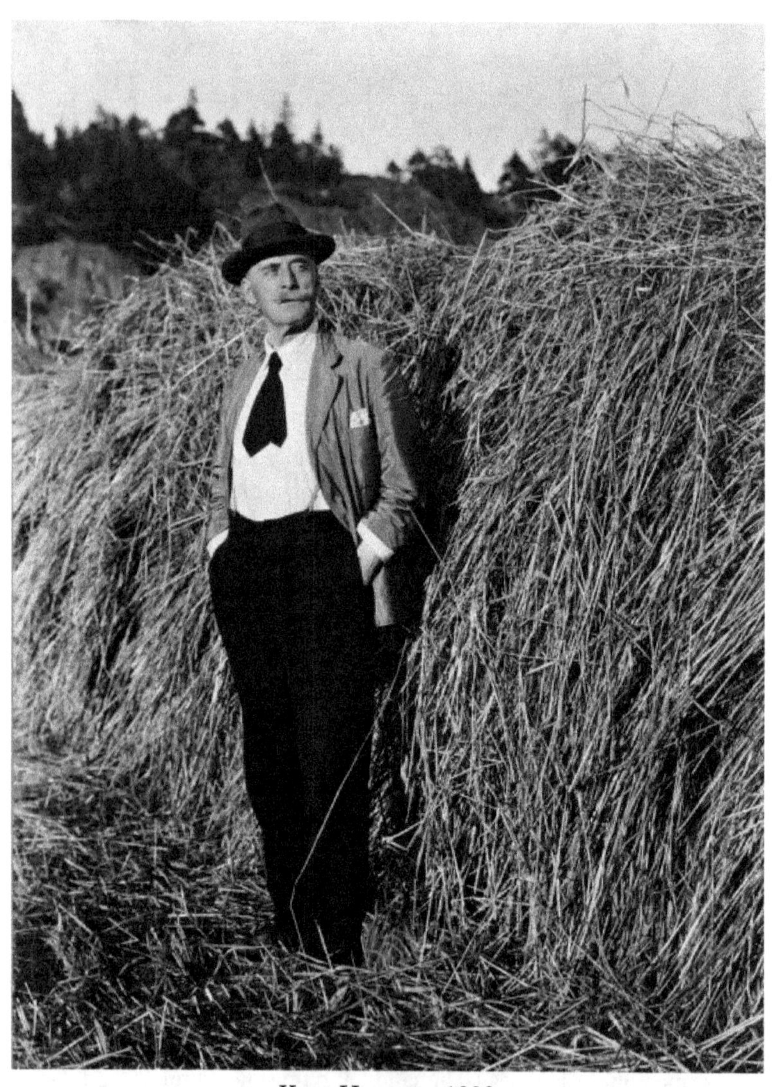

Knut Hamsun, 1930

becomes more effeminate and degenerate. A very demoral-
izing influence Hamsun sees in the tourist traffic of modern
times. A great deal of emphasis is placed on this topic.[1]

Indifference to, if not contempt for, all cultural values of
the present age is characteristic of [the governing nature of
the main characters]. Real grandeur and genuine beauty and
culture are not to be found in our times according to these
iconoclasts. The ruling spirit of the age, that of democracy,
is inimical to true culture, they hold, and the leaders of the
masses are destitute of originality, nobility, and greatness.
Democracy they regard with disgust, because of its real or
supposed tendency to reduce all men to a common level,
which, of necessity, spells mediocrity. Hence the contempt
of Hamsun's favorite type for the masses. There has been
an intimate connection between the rise of democracy and
industrialism. The organized industrial laborer is the chief
exponent of democracy; this is the main reason for the un-
favorable verdict pronounced upon our modern economic
development; that it has physical and moral decline in its
wake is another.

In their efforts to escape from the disconcerting turmoil of
life, Hamsun's heroes seek to achieve the closest communion
with nature in its more primitive state. Their love of nature,
as well as their other characteristics, they share with the author, who has remained ever loyal to it, though his attitude
towards it has undergone a certain change. All the earlier
works of Hamsun are highly subjective and full of personal
elements; Hamsun has depicted himself in them from many
different angles. That is one of the reasons why he, almost
without exception, chose a man for the central figure [...][2]

Hamsun's later writing has been seen—stylistically speaking—as a step
back from the assertive Modernism of *Hunger* and *Mysteries* (1892) and
as an embrace of "reactionary romanticism".[3] This makes the subject
and style of Hamsun's later work compatible with Nazi notions of invig-
orating Nordic literature, without ever depicting the archetypes found
in actual Nazi cultural production.

For Hamsun, industry, democracy,[4] and modernism are linked and
deleterious to the spirit of man, which is countered by the natural antith-
eses: ruralism, absence of politics and age-old bonds and customs. Of
Hamsun's Nobel Prize-winning novel *Growth of the Soil* (1917), Wiehr
commented that Hamsun "turned completely away from civilization
and to the most primitive conditions existing in Nordland."[5] The story

was set in the harshest of settings—the hardscrabble glacier-scoured valleys of Northern Norway. Yet commentators sometimes conflate the protagonists' situations with the author's, which leads to a misleading interpretation of Hamsun's life in relation to his fiction. Even before winning the prize, the novelist did not till the stony fields of the Nordland by day and write earnest tales of endurance by candlelight after dark. He had a wife and children, visited cities across Europe to lecture and receive awards, staying at the best hotels, with his activities tracked by the newspapers. Hamsun's consecutive homesteads were large concerns, worked by employees. He did, however, chop logs into his eighties, until he was crippled by his second stroke. Hamsun was relieved to win the Nobel Prize because he could use it to pay farmhands and creditors, clearing debts accumulated through hotel bills, lavish dining, hard drinking, and gambling in resort casinos. Author-as-ascetic is a construction grounded on the reality of the poverty of Hamsun's childhood and young adult life, one that was carefully tended in his writing. That is not to state that author-as-ascetic is always false—or even false in the case of Hamsun—just that it did not reflect the daily life of Hamsun when he wrote after 1890. Tied to the soil? Certainly, and devoted to it, but not exclusively a rural man. He wrote *Hunger* while a freelance journalist in Christiania, only recently returned from a sojourn in Chicago, and wrote early novels while living abroad in Copenhagen and Paris and while travelling on lecture tours.

Wiehr continues with his analysis of *Growth of the Soil*:

> In view of the didactic purpose of the novel, the stern truthfulness of the author is the more remarkable. How much more he could have ingratiated himself with many readers, if he had suppressed some of the more primitive features in the lives of these outposts of civilization. But Hamsun cannot find any satisfaction in mere imagined greatness, beauty, and virtue and he paints Isac and the rest 'wart and all.' His hero is truly great enough despite his limitations. He is a pioneer, body and soul, and a tiller of the soil who knows no resting from his labors. A figure resurrected from the past which points out the future, a man from the dawn of agriculture, a man seizing land (*Landnamsmand*), nine hundred years old and now again the man of the hour.[6]

By the late 1910s, most of Hamsun's income came from sales of his writings translated into German and he was held up as a standard-bearer for the vitality of Nordic culture and the Teutonic peoples, so Hamsun's esteem and income was in part derived from Germans. The reception of Hamsun's fiction by Nazi Germany as a manifestation of the Nordic spirit is extremely complicated and can only be glossed here. (Although I hope to discuss this at length in future.) There were obviously appealing characteristics of Hamsun's writing: the heroic protagonists overcoming adversity; the deprecation of cities and urban life; respect for the toil of the peasant; scepticism towards Christianity; contempt for bourgeois materialism; wholesale rejection of modernity, democracy, liberalism, and egalitarianism; finally (and most importantly) was an unwavering belief in a mystical bond between man and the land that formed a distinct Nordic national character. Rosenberg wrote,

> In the same medium *Hamsun*, in a mysterious natural insight, describes the laws of the universe and of the soul. Once again the characters are peasants, fishermen, merchants, in whom a world is reflected. Through travel, through unsatisfied longings, they lose contact with Mother Earth whose blessing is no longer with them. They move from place to place, exchanging activities and loving. But since the roots are torn out of the strength-giving earth, the blossoms also die. So they live their lives—Edevart, August, Lovise Margrets [of *Wayfarers*]—without knowing why and without direction. [...] Yet the Nordic spirit is never fully repressed or lost.[7]

Heidegger saw in Hamsun's characters evidence for the instability of existence in the face of the force of the world.[8] Heidegger, who thought of the world as understood through tool use and man's actions as constituting philosophical meaning, was naturally receptive to Hamsun's characters, who make meaning in their life through toil upon the soil. Heidegger would later retire to a Black Forest log cabin (*die Hütte im Schwarzwald*), a place of silence and site of contemplation, where he cut his own wood and drew water in a bucket. It was in Heidegger's 1950 book *Holzwege* (Wood Ways) that "The Origin of the Work of Art" was first published.

Beyond the subject matter and themes of his writing, Hamsun's politics aligned with Nazi Germany. He was virulently anti-British and (to a lesser extent) anti-American;[9] he backed Germany during World War I (contrary to elite consensus in Norway at the time); he opposed the Versailles Treaty that humiliated Germany; he welcomed the appointment of Hitler as Chancellor and publicly endorsed Nazi values; he supported Nasjonal Samling (the far-right party of Norway) in 1936;[10] he did not oppose the invasion of Norway by Germany in 1940; he backed the Quisling puppet government. Hamsun met many Nazi officials, dined with Goebbels, and had an audience with Hitler. His wife Marie toured German cities during World War II, offering her husband's public greetings to the German people. Rosenberg acclaimed Hamsun on his eightieth birthday as "the great creator of Nordic characters, and a stalwart friend of the new Germany." Going on to say, "Just as you created your characters for the world out of an indestructible will, you have released many similar feelings in the German people and given German literature life-giving impulses."[11]

So, on personal and political levels—as well as in literary terms—Hamsun's fortunes were tied to Romantic nationalism and veneration of the Nordic national character, most specifically and latterly in concert with Nazi ideology. Nazis (and the author himself) were willing to overlook a few incompatible marginal aspects of Hamsun's writing because in overall terms Hamsun's writings, reputation and active support was beneficial to the Nazis, who lacked the backing of many prestigious non-German creative figures. The existence of newly created popular, acclaimed body of work endorsing the uniqueness and vitality of Northern European people was taken as proof that National Socialism had spiritual, as well as literary, substance.

The prosecution of Hamsun by Norwegian authorities in 1945 (and again in 1947), following the defeat of Nazi Germany and the ending of its occupation of Norway, was a symbolic purging of Nordic nationalism as well as of Nazi collaborators. It was the drawing of a line that separated post-war Norwegian society from military defeat, foreign occupation and nationalism grounded in racial character. Hamsun was acquitted of treason in the first trial, due to old age and apparent decline in faculties. Apart from deafness, Hamsun's faculties were unimpaired, as was proved by him writing a last novel of high quality during the years he was supposedly mentally diminished. The point was to use the prosecution as a symbolic punishment—shaming without any intention of imposing a severe penalty. It was the Norwegian establishment expressing disapproval of Nordic nationalism and exculpating itself from indirectly inspiring or contributing to the Nazi project of racial supremacy. The conviction and subsequent fining of Hamsun in 1947 for his support of Nasjonal Samling seems to confirm this reading.

# ENDNOTES

1   Wiehr, 1922, p. 85.

2   Wiehr, 1922, pp. 121–2.

3   Sjølyst-Jackson, 2010, p. 10.

4   Hamsun had publicly spoken against democracy in lectures as early as 1891. Sjølyst-Jackson, 2010, pp. 43–4.

5   Wiehr, 1922, p. 104.

6   Wiehr, 1922, p. 112.

7   Rosenberg, 1930, quoted in Sjølyst-Jackson, 2010, pp. 117–8.

8   Sjølyst-Jackson, 2010, pp. 118–9.

9   See Hamsun, *From the Cultural Life of Modern America* (1889); for his racial antipathy towards black Americans, see Sjølyst-Jackson, 2010, p. 16.

10   "Its main goal was to overcome class tensions and unite the nation around a set of values and symbols, to establish a corporatist system of governance and to combat Bolshevism. The idea of a superior Nordic race played an important role in the ideology of the NS." Kyllingstad, 2014, ch. 9. There are differing views as to whether Hamsun was a member of Nasjonal Samling or just a supporter of it.

11   Alfred Rosenberg, 1939, quoted in Kolloen, 2009, p. 257.

# GERMAN ANTI-MODERNIST ART BEFORE 1933

Before the rise of the Nazi government, there existed strong cultural fault lines in the German art world. Traditionalist-nationalist painter Bettina Feistel-Rohmeder (1873–1953) had a "concept of a pure German art grounded in racial precepts [that] was firmly in place by 1905,"[1] when she attended a lecture by Henry Thode, who warned of the dangers of foreign art and modernism. Thode was a nationalist and anti-Modernist but not a strictly aesthetically conservative, as he adulated Böcklin.[2] Thode's leading public opponent was German Impressionist Max Liebermann, both a Modernist and Jewish. One attendee of Thode's lecture recalled, "one recognized immediately: this was a matter of life and death. Two life principles met each other in battle, Jewish-international liberalism and German nationalism."[3] Already by 1911, petitions against Modernism were circulating in the German art world.[4]

In 1920 Feistel-Rohmeder founded the German Art Society (Deutsche Kunstgesellschaft) in Dresden. In 1927, partly for financial reasons, the German Art Society became an affiliate of the ultra-nationalist German League (Deutschbund). Feistel-Rohmeder would become (by 1929) a member of the Nazi Party. "[Feistel-]Rohmeder was convinced that Jewish dealers, critics, and artists had infiltrated German culture in order to destroy the healthy sensibilities and racial identity of the Volk. Only the coordinated efforts of a *Völkisch* elite, a community of racially enlightened experts and activists, offered any chance of salvation."[5] She drew ideas of culture as emanating from race from the writings of Hans Friedrich Günther, Friedrich Wilhelm Prinz zur Lippe and Ludwig Ferdinand Clauss. Response to art was race recognition, which required racial consciousness.[6]

The German Art Society became a focal point for German artists who disliked Modernism and resented the (supposedly) favourable treatment received by Modernists and the Bauhaus. The activity of the Modernist-teaching, foreign-influenced, egalitarian Bauhaus art school had already aroused animosity from traditionalists and nationalists. Its socialist sympathies and links to Bolshevik art schools in the USSR made Bauhaus seem an active danger to Germany. In periodical articles, Feistel-Rohmeder opposed government support for foreign, Jewish, and Modernist artists during the Depression:

> [She] indignantly noted that Ludwig Justi, the Berlin National Gallery's director, sought to purchase a painting by Vincent van Gogh for 249,000 RM. Rather than pay such enormous sums of money for a painting by a deceased 'French' painter, Feistel-Rohmeder demanded that the funds be used to support living, contemporary (as opposed to modernist) German artists. Many artists were outraged by this purchase, including the 2,300 members of the National Association of Germany's Visual Artists in the Munich region.[7]

When the Nazis came to power in Germany in 1933, they had definite ideas on what culture they opposed (formed by political necessity and temperamental aversion) and had as their willing partner the German Art Society, which was already dedicated to advancing art that was Germanic in subject, style and personnel. The society's annual touring exhibition of German art would become the template for the *Große Deutsche Kunstaustellung* (*Great German Art Exhibition*), which would ultimately replace it. However, in the early years of the Nazi era, there was a struggle within the party over what was truly Germanic in culture.

One casualty was Liebermann, who resigned his position as president of the Prussian Academy, writing, "It is my conviction that art has nothing to do with politics or origin. Since this belief is no longer valid, I can no longer belong to the Prussian Academy [...]"[8] One newspaper responded, "Liebermann's idea about the isolated artist, alienated from the *Volkstum* [folk culture], has lost its validity today and in the future."[9]

# ENDNOTES


1    Clinefelter, 2005, p. 7.

2    Clinefelter, 2005, p. 9.

3    Edgar Schindler, quoted in Clinefelter, 2005, p. 12.

4    That of Carl Vinnen, 1911, signed by 134 artists. Adam, 1992, p. 29.

5    Clinefelter, 2005, p. 13

6    "How do we know if an artwork is German? That is not even the first question that we are dealing with here. Rather, [the question] is: are *you* German? That is, do you have the clear perception that everything our immortals have given us runs through you like a lively stream, that your essence cannot help but pulse and flow with this primal (*urgewaltigen*) river? If you are German in *this* way, then you do not need to ask [this question] even when you stand before a new piece of art; you already *know*!" Fesitel-Rohmeder, 1932, quoted in Clinefelter, 2005, p. 20.

7    Clinefelter, 2005, p. 51.

8    Quoted in Adam, 1992, p. 60.

9    *Tägliche Rundschau*, 11 May 1933, quoted in Adam, 1992, p. 60.

# NAZI RESPONSES TO ROMANTICISM

We only need to take a look at the material that was burned in the famous book-burning at Platz am Opernhaus (since renamed Bebelplatz), Berlin on 10 May 1933, to see what the Nazis opposed. Books and manuscripts from the nearby Humboldt University library and the Institute for Sexual Research were carried by students across Unter den Linden to the square in front of the opera house, where they were burned. The material fell into particular categories. The authors and subjects were classed as contrary to national interests, divided into groups that were political (liberal, Socialist, Communist, Marxist), subversive (anarchist, Freemasonic), deviant (psychiatric, psychoanalytic, sexology), immoral (pornography), racial (Jewish) and unpatriotic (anti-German, pacifist). Modernist culture was often seen as spanning multiple categories and treated accordingly.

The Nazis were convinced that the excesses of decadence during the Weimar Republic were the product of *Kulturbolschewismus* (German: cultural Bolshevism) and this could only be reversed by a nationalistic Aryan-led cultural revival, imposed from the top level of society. Consequently, the Bauhaus was closed permanently in 1933. The Kampfbund für deutsche Kultur (Militant League for German Culture), a Nazi body, declared its aims as "the goal of enlightening the German people about the connections between race, art, science, and moral and military values".[1] In 1937, the Ministry for Education and Science published a pamphlet declaring, "Dadaism, Futurism, Cubism, and other isms are the poisonous flower of a Jewish parasitical plant, grown on German soil [...] Examples of these will be the strongest proof for the necessity of a radical solution of the Jewish question."[2]

The racial interpretation of artistic capacity of peoples was set out by

Paul Schultze-Naumburg in *Kunst und Rasse* (Art and Race) (1928)—a book that influenced Feistel-Rohmeder. The book begins by examining the art and architecture of the Germans, using many comparative images, then it moves to the Greeks. The final section examines Modernist art with comparative images of Expressionist art and medical photographs of persons with physical deformities. The author explains that racially pure peoples produce clear, healthy, and great art, while racially impure (and inferior) races produce art that is unclear, unhealthy, and weak, and that Modernist art is made by, emulated from, collected by and promoted by racially impure and consequently degenerated individuals. It is in this book (republished for a third time in 1938) that we find assertions regarding artistic degeneracy and apparent physiological and racial degeneracy that appeared (paraphrased) in Nazi captions used in the touring *Entartete Kunst* (*Degenerate Art*) exhibition, which opened in Munich in 1937. Feistel-Rohmeder had a hand in suggesting and arranging various exhibitions of "degenerate art" across Germany. Schultze-Naumburg's racial attitudes have been summarised thus: "Schultze-Naumburg was convinced that 'blood and soil' are the 'two forces […] from which all other human artistic activity grows' and race had to be understood as 'a group of people with physical and mental qualities.'"[3] Rosenberg followed Schultze-Naumburg in these thoughts. In 1930, Paul Schultze-Naumburg was appointed head of the State Academy for Architecture, Crafts and the Visual Arts in Weimar and Interior and Culture Minister for Thuringia when the Nazis won power in that region, where he would carry out a campaign of anti-Modernism.

Adolf Hitler defined the purpose of art in the new National Socialist Germany in 1933:

> I am on the contrary convinced that art, since it forms the most uncorrupted, the most immediate reflection of the life of the people's soul, exercises unconsciously by far the greatest direct influence upon the masses of the peoples, but always subject to one condition: that it draws a true picture of that life and of the inborn capacities of a people and does not distort them.[4]

When opening the *Große Deutsche Kunstaustellung* in 1937, Adolf Hitler criticised Modernist art. He explained how supporters of Modernism had advocated art as an outgrowth of technology and era, not out of land and people. He paraphrased the Hegelian argument that art was conditioned by historicity:

There was no longer any art of peoples or even of races, but only an art of the times. According to this theory, therefore, Greek art was not formed by the Greeks, but by a certain period which formed it as their expression. The same, naturally, was true of Roman art, which, for the same reasons, coincided only accidentally with the rise of the Roman empire. Again in the same way the more recent art epochs of humanity have not been created by the Arabs, Germans, Italians, French, etc., but are only appearances conditioned by time. Therefore simply only a "modern art." Consequently, art as such is not only completely isolated from its ethnic origins, but it is the expression of a certain vintage which is characterized today by the word "modern," and thus, of course, will be un-modern tomorrow, since it will be outdated.

Hitler went on to discuss culture as a product of race:

From the history of the development of our people we know that it is composed of a number of more or less differentiated races, which in the course of millenniums, thanks to the overwhelming formative influence of one outstanding racial core, resulted in that particular mixture which we see in our people today. This power, once capable of forming a people, and thus still today an active one, is contained here again in the same Aryan race which we recognize not only as the carrier of our own culture, but as that of the preceding cultures of antiquity as well. This particular type of composition of our national heritage conditions the versatility of our own cultural development just as much as it does the resulting natural kinship with those peoples and cultures of the same homogenous racial core in other European countries of the same family of peoples. Nevertheless, we who see in the German people the gradually crystallizing end result of this historical process, desire for ourselves an art which takes into account within itself the continually growing unification of this race pattern and, thus, emerges with a unified, well-rounded total character.

The question has often been asked: What does it really mean to be German? Among all those definitions which through the centuries have been suggested by many men, the most valuable one for me seems to be that one which from the start does not even try to give an explanation, but which rather sets up a law. And the most beautiful law which I can envisage for my people as the task set for its life in this

> world, a great German has already long ago put into words:
> 'To be German is to be clear.' This, moreover, implies that
> to be German means to be logical and also, above all, to be
> true [...]

Hitler went on to link the inaugural exhibition in Munich at the new Haus der Deutschen Kunst to the destruction of the Glaspalast museum, which destroyed many paintings by German Romantic masters.

> Now, this deep inner longing for such a true German art
> which carries within it the traits of this law of clarity has al-
> ways been alive in our people. It occupied our great painters,
> our sculptors, the formers of our architecture, our thinkers
> and poets, and probably to the highest degree, our musicians.
> When on that fateful 6th of June in 1931 the old *Glaspalast*
> burnt down in that horrible fire, an immortal treasure of
> such true German art went up in flames. They were called
> the Romantics, but in essence they were the most glorious
> representatives of those noble Germans in search of the true
> intrinsic virtue of our people and the honest and respectable
> expression of those only inwardly experienced laws of life.
> Yet it was not only the chosen subject matter that was deci-
> sive for the characterization of the German substance, but
> just as important was the clear and simple manner in which
> these feelings were represented [...][5]

There was an internal debate within the Nazi Party regarding what should be classed as "degenerate" and what approved. There was a traditionalist wing that backed art that was realistic or idealistic, centred on rural subjects, Germanic landscape and people, that was conventional. This was opposed by a group that considered themselves more urbane and artistically adventurous (including Goebbels among their number) who wanted to include more Modernist art, including Expressionist painting and prints, which drew upon a vitalist racial strand of nationalism that reflected the supposed rawness and strength of the Nordic character.[6] This art would have given Nazism a link to art via elemental essence, as opposed to the more cultivated (even neutered) fussiness of Biedermeier and Neo-Classicism associated with Germanic fine art, that the traditionalist Nazis preferred. Even Rosenberg admitted that some advanced art had good qualities. Impressionism was originally "borne by strong, talented artists" but "became a battle-cry of decomposing intellectualism."[7] He wrote that Expressionism had been diverted from its potential. "[I]nstead of nurturing a new style-constructing strength, it continued the process of atomization. Internally unprincipled [the Expressionists] devoured 'primitive art', over-reached themselves in praise of Japan and China, and began in all seriousness to direct European-Nordic art back to Asia."[8] The impingement of intellectualism and race-mixing confused and misdirected movements begun with genuine originality and value.

In a study of Rosenberg, James B. Whisker characterises him as the leading traditionalist Nazi:

> Rosenberg was wholly loyal to Adolf Hitler, but he conflicted on major points with others in Hitler's camp. His feud with Doctor Paul Josef Göbbels is almost legendary, and cannot wholly be reconciled within standard National Socialist thought. It struck at the bases of the new state system. Where Göbbels favoured a modern, concentrated, industrial state, Rosenberg preferred a rural, medieval, dispersed society.[9]

Whisker writes of Rosenberg's visual arts policy,

> Germanic art is close to, but still different from, Nordic Greek art in the pre-contamination years.[10] It seeks the ideals of beauty, heroism, courage, harmony, truth and so on. It rejects impressionism, cubism, and similar modern art forms. These are incompatible with, and alien to, the Germanic folkish culture. Rosenberg was concerned both with form and with subject. He was not so blatant as some of his contemporaries, notably Mussolini in Italy, in demanding that art show Hitler, the S.S., the S.A., and other political themes. He did demand respect for the past and for heroes capable of forming types. He also demanded that heroes be depicted with Nordic features, and that symbols of evil be shown with features of alien races, especially Jews. Art was to convey impressions of the Myth and of the folk. It was to reinforce the ethic and values reached elsewhere in his works.[11]

Rosenberg favoured Romanticism, seeing it as a naturally Germanic art form, once cleansed of some extraneous associations.[12] Hitler's support for Romanticism was signalled in a 1935 speech, in which he firmly rejected Nordic-vitalist aesthetics. "Art must be the Prophetess of Sublimity and Beauty and thus sustain that which is at once natural and healthy. The cult of the primitive is not the expression of a naïve unspoiled soul, but of utterly corrupt and diseased degeneracy."[13] The

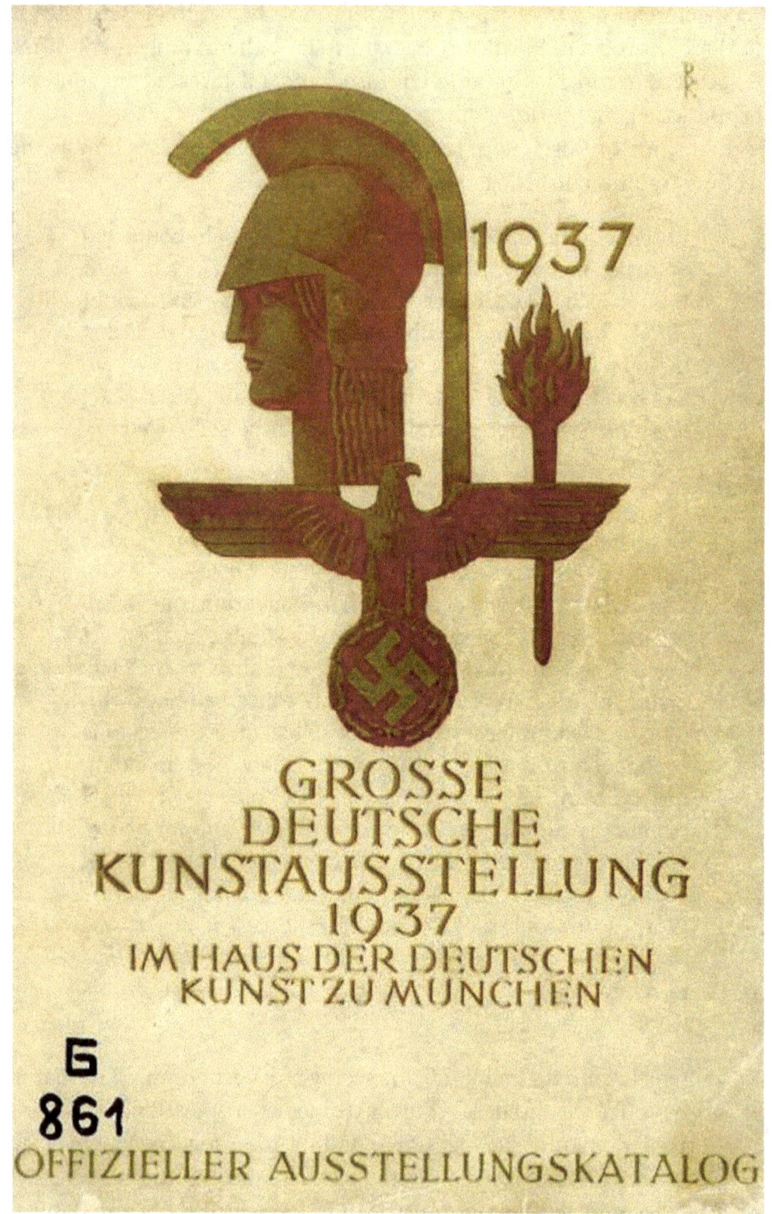



*Große Deutsche Kunstaustellung*, catalogue cover, 1937, Munich

traditionalists (headed by Hitler) carried the day and Romanticism, Naturalism, Heroic Realism and Neo-Classicism became the styles favoured by the Nazi authorities. There were room for differences even within the two camps. Schultze-Naumburg and Rosenberg rejected the Gothic as "decadent, a Jewish-Christian culture".[14]

Given the pronounced antipathy felt by Pan-Germanists towards the debasing and debilitating effect of urban life upon Germans, there was a strong preference for German nationalist art to depict rural and wild landscapes.[15] The landscapes of Friedrich became a template for spiritually charged nationalism. "It is no accident that [Friedrich's] rediscovery coincides with the beginning of the *martial saeculum*,[16] and that the pinnacle of his influence coincides with the outbreak of the World War. No accident, too, that since 1933 Caspar David Friedrich's effect has begun to grow."[17] As Friedrich had painted *Ulrich von Hutten's Grave* (1823–4), which showed a lone soldier contemplating the neglected grave of a patriotic German historian, so it was reasonable to ascribe to the painter a degree of nationalist sentiment. We are invited to identify with the *Rückenfiguren* (German: rear-facing figures) who stand in the foreground of Friedrich's landscapes and contemplate nature, ruins and the infinite; these figures often wear German clothing, already considered archaic by Friedrich's time. The combination of symbolism, idealism, patriotism, and nativism made Friedrich's art amenable for stewards of German art during the Nazi epoch.

During the selection of the exhibits for the first *Große Deutsche Kunstaustellung*—within which Hitler participated,[18] alongside a jury of experts—Goebbels (in his private diary) admits it was a struggle to find suitable art works to fill the new museum,[19] designed by architect Paul Troost (1878–1934).[20] It seems there was no stylistic criteria for selection, simply an effort to find art that was stylistically conservative and competent.[21] The difficulties Nazi culture faced are exemplified by the fact that in 1936 Goebbels banned art criticism from the press. "From now on art reporting will take the place of art criticism."[22]

What did Nazi-approved art look like? This is a reasonable question, because relatively little of it has been published or exhibited since 1945. A mixture of inaccessibility, shame, and taboo—combined with an unexamined consensus that the material was just too mediocre to warrant consideration—has kept the art out of sight.[23] We find some traditional genres, with some works directed towards political ends. There are many landscapes of Germany, primarily scenes of rural land and wild terrain, indistinguishable from landscape painting of different eras and countries but with patriotic titles referring to the Fatherland and na-

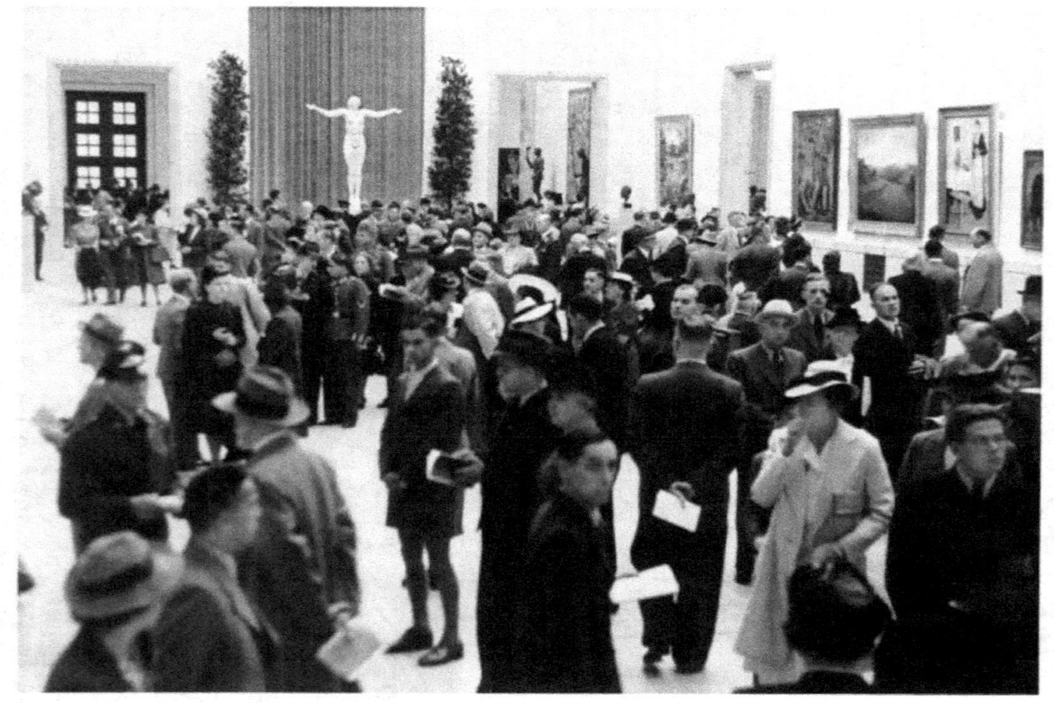

Große Deutsche Kunstaustellung, Munich, 1937

tional symbols. Peasants were often portrayed. Some 40% of the art in the *Große Deutsche Kunstaustellung* were landscapes.[24] Hitler became a major personal patron of painting, buying 202 paintings from the second *Große Deutsche Kunstaustellung*, and acquiring nearly 1,000, which he donated to public buildings and government offices. He understood the imprimatur of the label "Purchased by the Führer" and expected this would help the careers and incomes of favoured artists.[25]

German painter Sepp Hilz (1906–1967)[26] made his celebrated *A Peasant Venus* (1939?) showing a country girl undressing in old-fashioned bedroom, equating the goddess of love and beauty to the simple and natural German woman. At once, it elevated the local and did away with the need for a Greek archetype. Nudes were more common in Nazi art than Soviet art, because of the centrality of the doctrines of racial homogeneity and superiority of the Aryan/Nordic race in both politics and culture in Germany, as well as a lingering desire to associate Nazi art with classic art of the past. There are many pictures of maternity and suckling infants, more than one finds in Soviet art. These translated well into posters, which are more didactic than Nazi fine art. Heroic Realism of the Soviet and Nazi art—featuring rural workers, manual workers, children in organised activity, athletes and the military—made in painting, mural, sculpture and mosaic forms, are scarcely distinguishable from one another.[27] Likewise, the heroic, legible and stylistically conservative paintings of leaders, political martyrs and scenes of recent history are identical in Nazi Germany and the USSR, with only the clothing and political symbols indicating the ideology presiding.[28] The monumental statuary of Germany (not least, that made for the 1936 Olympic Games) followed the example set out by Fascist civic statuary.

Neutral subjects such as marines, still-lifes, and portraits continued unaffected. Abstract, Modernist, and anti-patriotic art was banned from public display; socialist, Communist, Jewish, and otherwise disapproved-of artists found opportunities curtailed. Notably, Nazi fine art did not portray the "inferior" races or political opponents—outside of some battle pictures—only showing them in posters, film, and other propaganda. It seems both the Nazi Party and fine artists had an aversion to sullying art spaces and high art status with images that were unbecoming. Fine art was for the promotion of Germanic art on Germanic subjects.

One of the artists most championed by the Modernist-supporting reactionary Nazi faction was Munch.[29] Munch was highly regarded in Germany, following his ground-breaking work made and exhibited in

Berlin in the 1890s. There were many works by him in German museums by 1932, when President Hindenburg presented him the Goethe Medal.[30] When the Nazi official consensus backed traditionalism, Munch and the Expressionists were classed as degenerate and their art put into storage or deaccessioned *en masse*.[31] Eighty-two works by Munch in German public collections were confiscated and sold by the Nazi authorities.[32] When it came to occupation of Norway, Munch was not harmed or molested but he rejected the Nazi and Quisling authorities. Contrast this with Hamsun's public support for the Nazis. Munch's art was included in an exhibition of approved art, arranged by the Quisling occupation government in April 1942 at the Nasjonalmuseet, Oslo, and articles favourable to the artist were published in Norwegian- and German-language newspapers for circulation in occupied Norway.[33]

Ultimately, Hitler's preference for Neo-classicism in architecture and the Romantic in art[34] would win out over the Nordic-vitalist strain in Nazism and would become official policy by 1935.

ENDNOTES

1    Quoted in Peters, 2014, p. 22.

2    Quoted in Adam, 1992, pp. 12–5.

3    Mario-Andreas von Lüttichau, in Olaf Peters, 2014, p. 22.

4    Hitler, quoted in Golomstock, p. 184.

5    Hitler, "Speech inaugurating the "Great Exhibition of German Art 1937," Munich"", in Herschel B. Chipp (*ed.*), *Theories of Modern Art*, University of California Press, Berkeley, 1968, pp. 476–9.

6    "[O]n 29 June [1933] the National Socialist German Student League of Berlin hosted a public meeting at the Humboldt University and openly declared its support for the 'Nordic' Expressionists, including Ernst Barlach, Emil Nolde, Ernst Heckel and Karl Schmidt-Rottluff." Clinefelter, 2005, p. 70, see also pp. 70–4.

7    Rosenberg, 1937, quoted in Harrison, 2003, p. 412.

8    Rosenberg, 1937, quoted in Harrison, 2003, p. 413.

9    James B. Whisker, in Rosenberg, 1937, unpag.

10    Rosenberg considered the Greeks and the Nordic peoples as originally linked as pure Aryan races and thus, before German emulation of culture of the Romance nations, Nordic art was a branch of Greek classical art. This position was set out by Hitler in *Mein Kampf*, 1925–6.

11    James B. Whisker, in Rosenberg, 1937, unpag.

12    "The reaction in the form of German romanticism was therefore as welcome as rain after a long drought. But in our own era of universal internationalism, it becomes necessary to follow this racially linked romanticism to its core, and to free it from certain nervous convulsions which still adhere to it. The Germanic peoples have not developed on the basis of some nebulous goal proffered by priests or scholars, but have either asserted themselves, or have disintegrated and been subjugated." James B. Whisker, in Rosenberg, 1937, unpag.

13    Hitler, 1935, quoted in Adam, 1992, p. 12.

14    Adam, 1992, p. 27.

15    Clinefelter, 2005, p. 62.

16    Latin: the point of commencement of a generational renewal.

17    A German art critic, quoted in Koerner, 2009, second edition, ch. 4.

18    "Hitler himself stepped in and rejected 80 pictures as 'unfinished.'" Adam, 1992, p. 95.

19    Clinefelter, 2005, p. 101.

20    Notably, Troost was an exponent of Modernism not Neo-classicism, although he adapted his style for Nazi-commissioned buildings. Hitler considered Troost "the greatest German architect since the nineteenth-century Neoclassicist Karl Friedrich Schinkel." Adam, 1992, p. 211.

21    See Olaf Peters, pp. 106–125, in Peters, 2014, esp. pp. 108–110.

22    Goebbels, quoted in Adam, 1992, p. 69.

23    Adams, 1992, pp. 7–9.

24    Adam, 1992, p. 97.

25    Adam, 1992, p. 115.

26    Hitler paid a generous sum directly from himself for the building of a new studio. Adam, 1992, p. 116.

27    For a description of National Socialist public art in military and civilian settings in Norway, see Stratigakos, 2022, ch. 3. Adam (1992, p. 204) notes that Soviets retained monumental statues by leading Nazi sculptor Arno Breker, suggesting a correlation.

28    For a discussion about the roles of women in Soviet and Nazi art, see Alexander Adams, *Women and Art: A Post-Feminist View*, Imprint Academic, Washington DC, 2022, pp. 213–237.

29    Goebbels to Munch, 1933: "Greatest Painter of the Germanic World [...] Sprouted from Nordic-Teutonic soil, his works speak to me of life's profound seriousness. His paintings, landscapes as well as representations of human beings are suffused by deep passion. Munch struggles to comprehend nature in its truth and to capture it in the picture, uncompromisingly scorning all academic formality. A powerful, independent strong-willed spirit-heir of Nordic culture—he frees himself of all naturalism and reaches back to the eternal foundations of National art-creating." Quoted in Prideaux, 2005, pp. 312–3.

30    Prideaux, 2005, p. 311.

31    A photograph of paintings including those by Munch can be found in Peters, 2014, p. 247.

32    Prideaux, 2005, p. 311. Four of the 13 most valuable degenerate paintings sold by the Nazis in May 1938 were by Munch.

33    Stratigakos, 2022, pp. 12–3

34    Hitler was an admirer of Hans Makart, Anselm Feuerbach, Ferdinand Waldüller. Adam, 1992, p. 43.

# DIE TOTENINSEL

Most of Berlin's museums are concentrated on Museumsinsel, a narrow island that is the site of the Berliner Dom, Böde Museum, Pergamon Museum, Neues Museum, Alte Nationalgalerie and the new museum built on the site of the since-demolished Königlisches Schloß, set around the Lustgarten, a park within which stands a giant granite bowl. On the first floor of the Alte Nationalgalerie is an oil painting on a wooden panel measuring 80 x 150 cm, catalogue number 2/80. In it an island forms a broken cup of stone, within which nestles a copse of cypresses, dark against pale greys and browns of bare rock. Partially concealed by the trees and set into the inward-facing cliff faces are tombs. A low wall at the front of the isle is divided by a set of stone steps that lead to the water, water which reaches the edges of the picture and to the horizon. Approaching the island is a bark in which a waterman conveys towards the steps a draped coffin and a standing figure covered head to toe in white. The figures are seen from behind. The sky is cloudy, and the water, be it lake or sea, is unsettled but not heavy. The lighting is diffuse, the time of day indeterminate.

The sea and sky are the same tone and hue, with the horizon merely implied. This gives the central motif separateness. It appears to float, unanchored in space. This is a painting with no foreground. The boatman is in a very curious position, half standing, leaning forward. He is apparently rowing, indicated by a faint handle line and the twin dashes of white water. It really is not possible to row in this position. Does the wake indicate that the man is rowing (truly impossible in the shown stance) or slowing the boat with the oars? That too seems unlikely because the heavy boat propelled by a single oarsman could hardly have built up sufficient speed to generate white water. Additionally, such an action could be just as easily—no, more easily—be performed by the

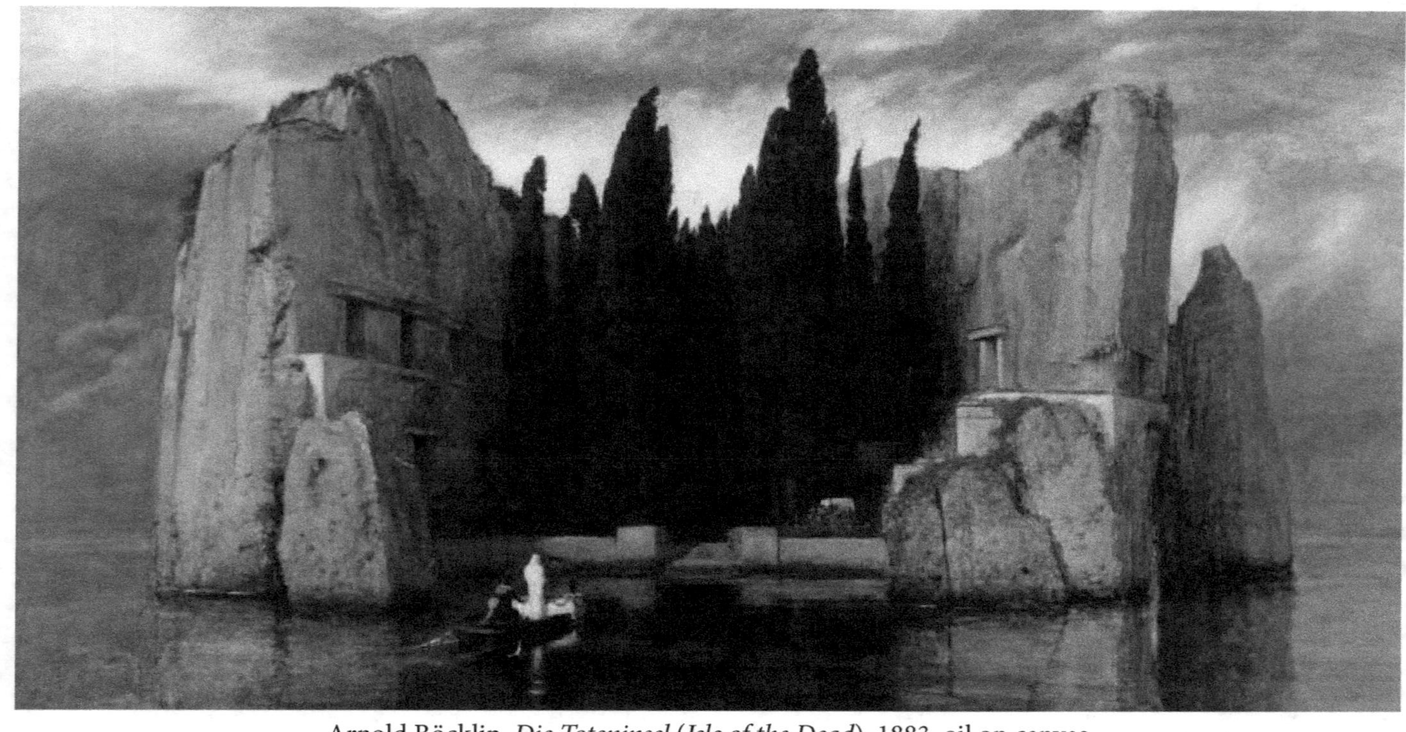

Arnold Böcklin, *Die Toteninsel (Isle of the Dead)*, 1883, oil on canvas

boatman in a seated position. Why is the boatman facing forwards—the wrong way? Paint is very lightly and loosely applied, especially on the rocks to the right of the isle. On the rock, oranges, violets and pinks are smudged. The greens of algae (at the water's edge) and moss (in the shade of the cypresses) are sharp and acidic against the heavy, earthy hue of the trees. The upper outline of the motif dips at the centre, drawing the eye to the centre of the painting, as does the direction of the boat, the perspective lines of the tomb lintels. Everything pulls the gaze to that dark centre and its Stygian cenotaph.[1]

It was painted in 1883 by Swiss Romantic-Symbolist artist Arnold Böcklin (1827–1901). The painter had secreted his initials in a way that was unobtrusive, turned into an inscription in the rock, almost suggesting that this was his tomb. The artist's initial titles *A Quiet Place* and *Cemetery Island* were supplanted by *Die Toteninsel* (*Isle of the Dead*). The artist painted five versions: the first two were painted in 1880 (one in New York, one in Basel); the third version is in Berlin; a fourth painting of 1884 ended up in Rotterdam (before its destruction during the World War II); a final variant of 1886 is now in Leipzig.[2] The five paintings were of roughly similar sizes and proportions, though the exact composition varies in each. Three were painted on wood, the Rotterdam version was painted on copper, one is on canvas. It is a fantasy but was drawn from observation of a real cemetery in Florence. The original painting with a funereal subject was requested by a grieving patroness.

*Die Toteninsel* became hugely famous. By the time of the artist's death, it was described as "perhaps more widely known than any other German work of art since the sixteenth century."[3] *Die Toteninsel* was reproduced in numerous prints—one executed by the notable German Symbolist Max Klinger—and illustrations in journals and books. As an iconic image of grief and duty, *Die Toteninsel* struck a chord (one both morbid and sentimental) with an international public. Not least, it was startling visually memorable and original. Sustaining its mystery, it failed to reveal its secrets upon scrutiny, instead inviting the viewer to engage in extended meditation upon mortality and mourning. Alongside Millet's *The Angelus* (1857–9) (an image of peasant piety), *Die Toteninsel* offered an alternative popular icon of spiritual reflection, albeit one that offered colder comfort. Its consolation was pre-Christian, with the isle's sheer cliffs forming a natural amphitheatre of pagan times, with the imagery harkening back to that associated with Charon, boatman of the Styx, taking the bodies of the departed to Hades. The painting came to obsess Salvador Dalí; a version of it was painted by

Glenn Brown.

Later, Böcklin painted an antipolar counterpart. Entitled *Die Lebensinsel* (*The Isle of Life*) (1888), it shows figures in classical garb on a sunlit verdant isle; in the surrounding water are mermen, Nereids and waterfowl. Rather understandably, that painting left no mark on the public psyche.

Although Swiss-born, Böcklin was acclaimed as a Pan-German genius.[4] Rosenberg wrote (in 1930) of his admiration for the "powerful originality" of Böcklin, which "breaks forth eternally". He declared, "the Homeric destiny which had once been promised to Böcklin had already been decided. To hang the *Isle of the Dead* upon one's wall today has become an inward impossibility."[5] For Rosenberg, the idealism of Romantic fantasy had been undone by the relentless anti-mythical modernity of the twentieth century.

The Berlin version was commissioned by Fritz Gurlitt (1854–1893),[6] an art dealer born in Vienna but living in Berlin. The official catalogue of the Berlin museums notes the following: *1933 wurde diese Version auf dem Kunstmarkt angeboten und von Adolf Hitler erworben, der das Werk bewunderte. Er häugte es zunächst auf dem Berghof am Obersalzberg auf, ab 1940 in der Berliner Neuen Reichkanzlei* ["In 1933 this version was bought from the art market by Adolf Hitler. It hung in the Berghof in Obersalzberg and from 1940 in the New Reich Chancellery in Berlin"]. Long before the looting and extortion which amassed an incredible horde of art for a projected Reich art museum in Linz, the year he came to power Hitler bought the third version of Böcklin's masterpiece for himself. It is a strange thought that one of Romanticism's great and morbid masterpieces hung in the Reich Chancellery, the site of the planning of continental conquest, gazed upon by its architect. When the air raids on Berlin intensified, it was taken to the Führerbunker and was taken from there, after Hitler's death, to Moscow by the Soviet military as a trophy.

The painting now hangs in Berlin's Alte Nationalgalerie, where its provenance goes unmentioned in the wall label.

# ENDNOTES

1    See also "Die Toteninsel" in Alexander Adams, *On Art*, Golconda Fine Art Books, 2018.

2    "His first picture of this motive, dating from 1864, is in the Schack Gallery of Munich, another, of 1877, is in the Stuttgart Gallery, several others are in private collections [...]" Burroughs, 1926, p. 146. This is apparently a different composition.

3    Burroughs, 1926, p. 146.

4    "'Pan-German genius, with which, in literature, philosophy, and discoveries, only the Greeks could compete; whose music, as represented by Bach and Beethoven, has never been surpassed; that genius, to which the French are only superior in Cuvier, the Spaniards in Columbus, and the Poles in Copernicus, having always been beaten by Latin genius in the field of art has, in Böcklin, at length found a worthy champion. In him, German art has a great representative, whom the Germans admire, as the greatest poet-painter among them. He has succeeded in what Göthe strove in vain to accomplish, viz., he has grafted the German soul into the antique ideal of beauty. During a charming afternoon, on a certain summer day, he perceived old Pan, and through the medium of his glaring colours, he has restored to the Germans that which they had lost; their sentiment of universe and infinity.' Thus spoke proudly Ola Hanson of Böcklin. Unfortunately for Germans, Nietzsche says that Bocklin was not a German, and he exclaims:— 'What poets had Germany to equal the Swiss Keller? Has there ever been a scientist like Jacob Burkhardt? A path-finding painter like Böcklin?'" Count de Soissons, "Arnold Böcklin", *The Artist*, vol. 31, August 1901.

5    Rosenberg, 1937, unpag.

6    His son Fritz and nephew Hildebrand would become Nazi-favoured art dealers, handling looted and extorted art, in Berlin and Munich respectively.

# HEIDEGGER'S AESTHETICS

Providing a philosophical grounding for some aspects of Nazi policy and attitudes, is seen by some as partial motivation for "The Origin of the Work of Art", a lecture by the German philosopher Martin Heidegger (1889–1976). First delivered by Heidegger on 13 November 1935 at Freiburg University, the author later expanded the talk into three lectures, delivered at the end of 1936, and published them after the war.

Heidegger is credited as the most prominent thinker of the phenomenologist Continental School. He studied under Edmund Husserl, as did many important aesthetic theorists, ones who took contrary positions to him. Heidegger's phenomenology was distinct from (even in some sense opposed to) Husserl's, which in later stages inclined towards Neo-Kantianism. Heidegger was opposed to Neo-Kantian readings of aesthetics and had a conception of aesthetics that was cognitivist, not emotional—thought determined aesthetic reaction more than emotion. Heidegger wrote of his outlook on existence:

> Feeling, as feeling oneself to be, is precisely the way we are corporeally. Bodily being does not mean that the soul is burdened by a hulk we call the body. In feeling oneself to be, the body is already contained in advance in that self, in such a way that the body in its bodily states permeates the self. We do not 'have' a body in the way we carry a knife in a sheath. Neither is the body a natural body that merely accompanies us and which we can establish, expressly or not, as being also at hand. We do not 'have' a body; rather, we 'are' bodily. Feeling, as feeling oneself to be, belongs to the essence of such Being.[1]

In other words, the soul and body were one; likewise the body and mind are one, as is the body and the self.

Heidegger thought that aesthetic ideas since Friedrich Nietzsche (1844–1900) had not advanced and had become increasingly detached from the understanding and experience of common observers of culture.

> In recent decades we have often heard the complaint that the innumerable aesthetic considerations of and investigations into art and the beautiful have achieved nothing, that they have not helped anyone to gain access to art, that they have contributed virtually nothing to artistic creativity and to a sound appreciation of art. That is certainly true, especially with regard to the kind of thing bandied about today under the name 'aesthetics'. But we dare not derive our standards for judging aesthetics and its relation to art from such contemporary work. For, in truth, the fact whether and how an era is committed to an aesthetics, whether and how it adopts a stance toward art of an aesthetic character, is decisive for the way art shapes the history of that era—or remains irrelevant for it.[2]

Heidegger (as a phenomenologist) was concerned primarily with *Dasein* (German: "being there" or "presence"), which means a person existing in the world and experiencing it but feeling himself to be distinct or apart from the world. It is (in a very simplified way) similar to self-consciousness. Heidegger's *Dasein* in relation to art is also similar to Kant's conception of disinterested aesthetic appreciation:

> Parallel to the formation of aesthetics and to the effort to clarify and ground the aesthetic state, another decisive process unfolds within the history of art. Great art and its works are great in their historical emergence and Being (*Dasein*) because in man's historical existence they accomplish a decisive task: they make manifest, in the way appropriate to works, what beings as a whole are, preserving such manifestation in the work. Art and its works are necessary only as an itinerary and sojourn for man in which the truth of beings as a whole, i.e., the unconditioned, the absolute, opens itself up to him. What makes art great is not only and not in the first place the high quality of what is created. Rather, artis great because it is an 'absolute need.' Because it is that, and to the extent it is that, it also can and must be great in rank. For

only on the basis of the magnitude of its essential character does it also create a dimension of magnitude for the rank and structure of what is brought forth.[3]

Art is a primary means by which man can understand existence; art can reveal to man truths about himself. Art is not mental play, or really an expression of free will, but a device to record and communicate the truth.

We can find more of Heidegger's thoughts on aesthetics in his lectures and writings on Nietzsche. Heidegger noted the apparent contradiction in Nietzsche's philosophy of aesthetics. He saw Nietzsche's rejection of Idealism in favour of physiology as difficult to square with Nietzsche's aesthetics of truth—of art showing true things about human nature:

> Physiology knows no arena in which something could be set up for decision and choice. To deliver art over to physiology seems tantamount to reducing art to the functional level of the gastric juices. Then how could art also ground and determine the genuine and decisive valuation? Art as the counter-movement to nihilism and art as the object of physiology—that's like trying to mix fire and water. If a unification is at all possible here, it can only occur in such a way that art, as an object of physiology, is declared the utter apotheosis of nihilism—and not at all the counter-movement to it.[4]

Heidegger here says that physiology is necessarily subjective, because it varies between individuals' reactions, so using it as a measure of art is just turning aesthetics into a branch of biology. Art must express definite values, so it should not be measured in such a way. Despite holding Nietzsche in high esteem, Heidegger was troubled by Nietzsche's affinity for physiology in aesthetics. Nietzsche declared that he was in favour of fixed values and opposed to nihilism—a position that seems to contradict the subjectivity, individuality and reflexivity inherent in physiological interpretation of responses to art. Heidegger thought that the matter of aesthetics demanded a new approach.

# ENDNOTES

1   Heidegger, 1981, p. 99.
2   Heidegger, 1981, p. 79.
3   Heidegger, 1981, p. 84.
4   Heidegger, 1981, p. 93.

# THE ORIGIN OF
# THE WORK OF ART

Heidegger's most important writing on aesthetics is "The Origin of the Work of Art", the set of three lectures published in 1950. In this work, Heidegger identifies an unsatisfactory oddity of self-reference. "The artist is the origin of the work. The work is the origin of the artist. Neither is without the other."[1] The art work is art because it is made by an artist and an artist is an artist because he makes art. The very basic definitions we use in this case do not really explain anything: they simply describe the thing in terms of itself, and the maker in terms of his association with the activity or product.

Heidegger scholar David Farrell Krell summarised Heidegger's response to previous definitions of what an art work was:

> Heidegger begins by trying to identify the 'thingly' quality of artworks, as though 'thing' were the genus to which one would add the specific difference 'art' in order to make an artistic thing, i.e., a work. He examines three traditional interpretations of the 'thing' stemming from ancient ontology, (1) the thing as a substance to which various accidents or properties belong, or as a subject that contains certain predicates, (2) the thing as the unity within the mind of a manifold of sense-impressions, and (3) the thing as matter invested with form. But these interpretations reflect *their* origin in a particular kind of human activity, involvement with tools or equipment [...]; they therefore distort the character of both 'thing' and 'work'.[2]

Heidegger finds the first definition too general and accidental. The second definition is too much a matter of "something other is brought together with the thing that is made",[3] the art object as a "placeholder" for something more significant than itself. The third definition refuses to distinguish art from the general handiwork of mankind—obviously unsatisfactory for a philosopher who sees art as a unique channel for truth discovery.

Heidegger discusses the way things that are made to perform tasks—such as tools—should be considered incomplete in themselves because they lack the work or action that makes them useful. They are a subset of things. Is art equipment? Certainly, removed from context, certain equipment (like African religious fetishes or statuary used sustain the existence of an ancient Egyptian's soul) become repurposed as art by other cultures. To explain both the concept of a thing as equipment and the idea of art as means of discovering truth, Heidegger takes as his example Vincent van Gogh's oil painting on canvas, *Shoes* (1886; Van Gogh Museum, Amsterdam):

> From Van Gogh's painting we cannot even tell where the shoes stand. there is nothing surrounding this pair of peasant shoes in or to which they might belong—only an undefined space. There are not even clods of soil from the field or the field-path sticking to them, which would at least hint at their use. A pair of peasant shoes and nothing more. And yet. From the dark opening of the worn insides of the shoes the toilsome tread of the worker stares forth. In the stiffly rugged heaviness of the shoes there is the accumulated tenacity of her slow trudge through the far-spreading and ever-uniform furrows of the field swept by a raw wind. On the leather lie the dampness and richness of the soil. [...] This equipment belongs to the *earth*, and it is protected by the *world* of the peasant woman. From out of this protected belonging the equipment itself rises to its resting-within-it-self.[4]

For Heidegger, the simple toiling life of a peasant is embodied in this equipment; the equipment gives an insight into the daily life of a peasant. How did we come by this truth? Heidegger elaborates:

> The repose of equipment resting within itself consists in its reliability. Only in this reliability do we discern what equipment in truth is. But we still know nothing of what we first sought: the thing's thingly character. And we know nothing at all of what we really and solely seek: the workly character of the work in the sense of the work of art.

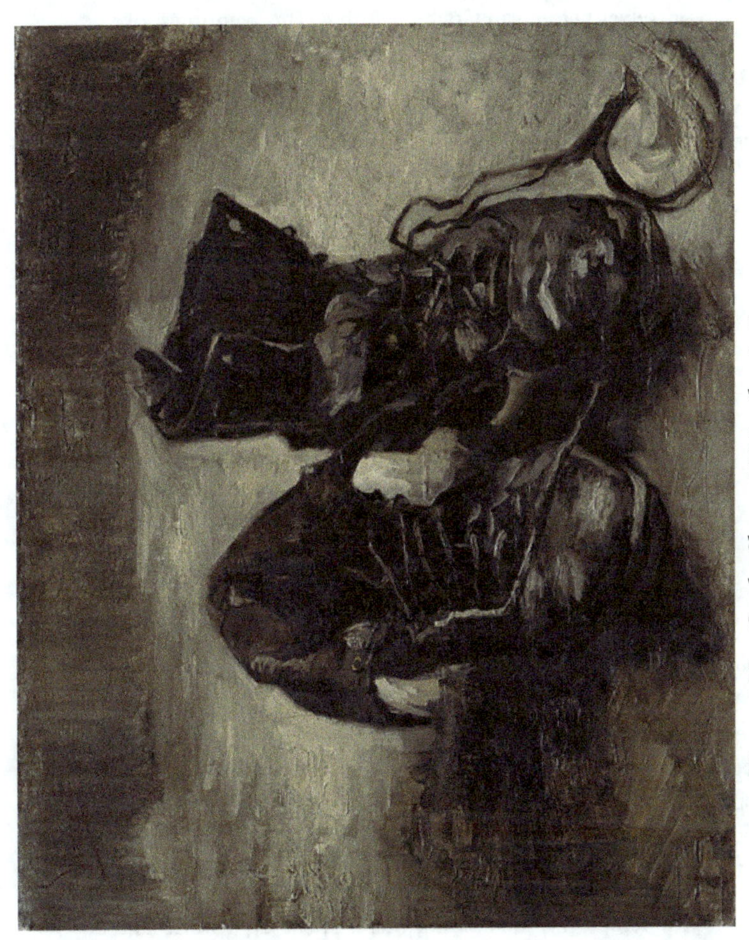

Vincent Van Gogh, *Shoes*, 1886, oil painting on canvas

"Or have we already learned something unwittingly—in passing, so to speak—about the work-being of the work?

"The equipmental quality of equipment was discovered. But how? Not by a description and explanation of a pair of shoes actually present; not by a report about the process of making shoes; and also not by the observation of the actual use of shoes occurring here and there; but only by bringing ourselves before van Gogh's painting. This painting spoke.[5]

So, the art work tells us a truth, in this case, about the experience of working in the fields, through the equipment of shoes. What makes art art? In a famous passage, Heidegger writes:

A building, a Greek temple, portrays nothing. It simply stands there in the middle of the rock-cleft valley. The building encloses the figure of the god, and in this concealment lets it stand out into the holy precinct through the open portico. By means of the temple, the god is present in the temple. This presence of the god is in itself the extension and delimitation of the precinct as a holy precinct. The temple and its precinct, however, do not fade away into the indefinite. It is the temple-work that first fits together and at the same time gathers around itself the unity of those paths and relations in which birth and death, disaster and blessing, victory and disgrace, endurance and decline acquire the shape of destiny for human being. The all-governing expanse of this open relational context is the world of this historical people. Only from and in this expanse does the nation first return to itself for the fulfillment of its vocation.[6]

Here Heidegger connects art, divinity, place, history and nationhood, suggesting that art draws its truth from the interconnection from all aspects. He follows this by stressing the importance of connection to rock and soil and its subsequent placeness and fixity. It emerges from earth, which is the substance of the planet and all that we know:

The temple-work, standing there, opens up a world and at the same time sets this world back again on earth, which itself only thus emerges as native ground. But men and animals, plants and things, are never present and familiar as unchangeable objects, only to represent incidentally also a fitting environment for the temple, which one fine day is added to what is already there.

This linkage has been seen as ideologically provocative, not least because this lecture was delivered by Heidegger while he was a member of the Nazi party. This was a circumstance that was used to attempt to discredit his aesthetics. What were those aesthetics? Heidegger's philosophy proposes creation more as a maker transmitting a received truth than active creation; aesthetic experience is truth reception, uninflected by mental play, imagination, or emotion in a cognitive process. Art springs from the people and place and is a means of discovering truth. As commentators such as Paul Guyer have observed, this model seems rather passive and mechanical.[7] A century earlier, Goethe went much further than Heidegger, asserting that the viewer lost his will in front of great art and that the artist imprinted his control on to his subject, regardless of volition on his part:

> The worst picture can speak to our perception and imagination, for it sets them in motion, makes them free, and leaves them to themselves. The best also speaks to our perception, but in a higher language, one, certainly, which has to be understood, but which chains our feelings and our imagination and robs us of our will-power, for we cannot do what we please with the perfect, we are compelled to surrender to it in order to receive ourselves again, raised and ennobled.[8]

In terms of aesthetic response, power politics and *zeitgeist*, the Nazis would have felt that Goethe's description matched their expectations of what a great man could do to a nation.

Artists and philosophers have responded to Heidegger's ideas on art but have struggled to do so without incorporating a political dimension into their assessments, failing to surmount the obstacle of the Nazi race ideology.

# ENDNOTES

1    Heidegger, 2008, p. 143.

2    Krell in Heidegger, 2008, pp. 140–1.

3    Heidegger, 2008, pp. 145–6.

4    Heidegger, 2008, pp. 159–160.

5    Heidegger, 2008, p. 161. Art theorist Meyer Schapiro criticised Heidegger's lectures on the basis that the boots in Van Gogh's paintings were not those of a peasant woman but the artist's own. Schapiro argued that if Heidegger asserted that truth could be ascertained from art, how could Heidegger's fundamental error not lead to consequential misleading assumptions? How truthful could any insights be, when they were founded on a misreading of the motif of a painting?

6    Heidegger, 2008, p. 167.

7    Paul Guyer, *A History of Modern Aesthetics, Volume 3*, Cambridge University Press, 2018, pp. 32–3 and pp. 41–2.

8    Goethe, quoted in Paul Guyer, *A History of Modern Aesthetics, Volume 1*, Cambridge University Press, 2018, p. 499.

# ARGUMENTS FOR
# AND AGAINST
# NATIONAL CHARACTER

Arguments have been advanced to suggest that racial classifications are too difficult to be exact and that therefore national character can only be cultural and environmental rather than genetic. Here is a typical argument, advanced in 1948:

> [E]very nation contains different racial elements, and is therefore mixed of different kins or breeds or stocks. You know a race—and this is its essence—by the common physical attributes of its members. It is a physical fact determined by physical factors of height and shape and colouring. If you adopt this zoological conception of race, you must recognize that each nation contains different races—long-heads as well as round-heads, and, again, tall and fair long-heads as well as long-heads who are short and dark. The soil of each country has been washed over again and again by different human species, which have left their representatives in its living population. France is the most homogeneous of nations; but in point of race, as we shall see, France is perhaps more composite than any other. It is indeed arguable, and it has been argued by Professor MacDougall, that the cross-breeding and blending of the different races of a given nation in the course of history may possibly produce a new 'sub-race,' fertile in reproduction and full of the fresh variations which the blending of different races makes possible. To admit such a possibility is, however, to open the door to confusion; and we shall only darken counsel by talk of a French or English sub-race. A race is a physical fact marked by physical fea-

tures; and we cannot find any physical features which mark the French as a single and united sub-race distinct from the English, On the contrary, the persistence of several different races alike in France and in England is an obvious fact; and the length of time that would be necessary to blend the different races of cither country into a new unity which abolished the old diversities (even if we assume for the moment that such a thing is now possible) is vastly greater than the period during which cross-breeding has been at work in any of the nations of Europe. We must abandon, therefore, any conception of the nation as a physical unity.[1]

One recent writer typifies modern academic attitudes on the subject, by describing national characterisations before dismissing them: "[T]he North is considered cool, frugal, cerebral, morally inclined and the South warm, sensual, opulent and immoral. This kind of environmental determinism is nowadays generally regarded as defunct, but it has exerted a powerful hold on the imagination."[2]

Prominent internationalists of the pre-World War II-period—H.G. Wells, George Orwell, George Bernard Shaw, the Fabian Society and others for example—admitted that national and racial characters existed, even if they went on to suggest ways of overcoming or eliminating such features. In public debate of the era, we find not a rejection of national character but an acceptance of it and (among liberalists, progressives and socialists) arguments about how best to compensate for national differences through humanist-materialist organisation, worldwide collaboration, the brotherhood of man, international socialism, technology, secularism and miscegenation. The foundation of the League of Nations, a series of peace congresses, the pacifism movement, the advancement of Esperanto and numerous other steps are evidence of acknowledgement of the existence of differences in national interest and outlook and the need to surmount them.

It is worth considering Wells on race, taken from his *Anticipations of the Reaction of Mechanical and Scientific Progress upon Human Life and Thought* of 1901:

> There are evident in Europe four or five or more very distinct racial types, and since the methods and rewards of barbaric warfare and the nature of the chief chattels of barbaric trade have always been diametrically opposed to racial purity, their original separation could only have gone on through such an entire lack of communication as prevented either trade or warfare between the bulk of the differentiating bod-

ies. These original racial types are now inextricably mingled. Unobservant, over-scholarly people talk or write in the profoundest manner about a Teutonic race and a Keltic race, and institute all sorts of curious contrasts between these phantoms, but these are not races at all, if physical characteristics have anything to do with race. The Dane, the Bavarian, the Prussian, the Frieslander, the Wessex peasant, the Kentish man, the Virginian, the man from New Jersey, the Norwegian, the Swede, and the Transvaal Boer, are generalized about, for example, as Teutonic, while the short, dark, cunning sort of Welshman, the tall and generous Highlander, the miscellaneous Irish, the square-headed Breton, and any sort of Cornwall peasant are Kelts within the meaning of this oil lamp anthropology. People who believe in this sort of thing are not the sort of people that one attempts to convert by a set argument. One need only say the thing is not so; there is no Teutonic race, and there never has been; there is no Keltic race, and there never has been. No one has ever proved or attempted to prove the existence of such races, the thing has always been assumed; they are dogmas with nothing but questionable authority behind them, and the onus of proof rests on the believer. This nonsense about Keltic and Teutonic is no more science than Lombroso's extraordinary assertions about criminals, or palmistry, or the development of religion from a solar myth. Indisputably there are several races intermingled in the European populations [...][3]

Wells goes on the write that just as racial types become mixed and homogenised within a continent, so differences in dialectic are erased through education, travel and centralised organisation. The process of mechanised mass communication, long-distance travel and standardisation of education lead to the suppression of dialects then later to the less common languages and the assimilation of difference. "And clearly this process of assimilation will continue. Even local differences of accent seem likely to follow."[4] When discussing diffusion of populations from country to town, Wells admits, "It is evident that from the outset racial and national characteristics will tell in this diffusion."[5] It becomes clear later that Wells did not deny the significance of racial differences: he simply classified races more broadly. Wells foresaw a global New Republic.

And how will the New Republic treat the inferior races? How will it deal with the black? how will it deal with the yellow man? how will it tackle that alleged termite in the civilized woodwork, the Jew? Certainly not as races at all. It will aim to establish, and it will at last, though probably only after a second century has passed, establish a world-state with a common language and a common rule. All over the world its roads, its standards, its laws, and its apparatus of control will run. It will, I have said, make the multiplication of those who fall behind a certain standard of social efficiency unpleasant and difficult, and it will have cast aside any coddling laws to save adult men from themselves. It will tolerate no dark corners where the people of the Abyss may fester, no vast diffused slums of peasant proprietors, no stagnant plague-preserves. Whatever men may come into its efficient citizenship it will let come—white, black, red, or brown; the efficiency will be the test. And the Jew also it will treat as any other man. It is said that the Jew is incurably a parasite on the apparatus of credit. If there are parasites on the apparatus of credit, that is a reason the legislative cleaning of the apparatus of credit, but is no reason for the special treatment of the Jew. If the Jew has a certain incurable tendency to social parasitism, and we make social parasitism impossible, we shall abolish the Jew, and if he has not, there is no need to abolish the Jew. [...] Much of the Jew's usury is no more than social scavenging. The Jew will probably lose much of his particularism, intermarry with Gentiles, and cease to be a physically distinct element in human affairs in a century or so. But much of his moral tradition will, I hope, never die [...] And for the rest, those swarms of black, and brown, and dirty white, and yellow people, who do not come into the new needs of efficiency?

Well, the world is a world, not a charitable institution, and I take it they will have to go. The whole tenor and meaning of the world, as I see it, is that they have to go. So far as they fail to develop sane, vigorous, and distinctive personalities for the great world of the future, it is their portion to die out and disappear.[6]

*Anticipations* was broadly welcomed by progressives upon publication and became a bestseller. It is an example of how progressive supporters of Social Darwinism (and eugenics) were those most inclined to support social engineering to combat and dissolve differences in racial physiognomy, ethnic culture and national traits—differences that they did not deny.

ENDNOTES

1    Ernest Barker, *National Character and the Factors in its Formation*, Methuen & Co., London, 1948 (1$^{st}$ edition 1927), p. 11.

2    Stougaard-Nielsen, 2020, p. 166.

3    Wells, 1902, pp. 217–8.

4    Wells, 1902, p. 226.

5    Wells, 1902, p. 56.

6    Wells, 1902, pp. 315–7.

# RACE AND DIFFERENCE

Having seen that national character was long acknowledged before World War II, often in a fairly uncontentious manner by individuals from differing political perspectives, sudden scepticism towards the existence of national character after 1939 seems all the more striking. Although there are a number of scientific, quasi-scientific and polemic studies of racial difference since World War II, it is necessary to only lightly touch upon a single post-war example of what race/ethnicity may mean for the grounding of national character. Richard Lynn's *Personality and National Character* (Pergamon Press, Oxford) was published in 1971. In the introduction, the author wrote that the field was indelibly marked by post-war animosity towards studies of racial difference but that nevertheless—or perhaps because of this—a scientific study of national characteristics was needed and feasible. Lynn described the general classifications within the white European group.

> Judged by observations, interviews and tests of personality, there appeared to be a well-marked contrast between the South European (or 'Mediterranean') type and the North European (or 'Nordic') type. The former seemed more sociable, loquacious, vivacious, and impulsive, their emotions were promptly and freely expressed, and as quickly subsided. The latter seemed to be more reserved, self-sufficient, self-assertive, and self-controlled; they were characterised by greater independence and individuality—eager to explore, investigate, and decide for themselves; their emotions were equally strong, but more firmly repressed and far more persistent. The mid-European (or 'Alpine') type seemed on the whole more phlegmatic than either of the two—slower and more conservative, yet at the same time shrewd and

> secretive, and (in many of my own cases) marked by strong
> aesthetic interests—a love of art and music.[1]

How do ethnic/racial traits relate to creativity? Lynn writes the following about an apparent correlation between anxiety and creativity:

> [I]t is shown that there is a strong tendency for the more anxious countries to have high growth rates. It is suggested that one reason for this may be that more anxious people work longer hours. Another possibility is that anxious people tend to be creative, and that the canalisation of creativity into business enterprises could result in a high rate of economic growth.[2]

Lynn provides statistics that rank nationalities from most anxious to least anxious. Readers are invited to consider this list in relation to the relative creativity expressed by the residents of these countries. Most anxious to least anxious: Austria, Japan, Germany, France, Denmark, Belgium, Switzerland, Norway, Finland, Sweden, the USA, Australia, the Netherlands, Canada, New Zealand, the UK, Ireland.[3] Is the difference in anxiety to do with the conditions or the traits of the people? Lynn writes,

> At the present stage, it would seem probable that both a racial and a climatic factor are required to explain the national differences in anxiety. [...] But the racial thesis advanced in the present chapter also fits a number of the facts.[4]

Breaking down the general racial groups into detailed race classification allows the prediction (or at least correlation to) levels of anxiety. University students from Europe were measured for self-reported anxiety. The highest-anxiety group included the nationalities Austria, Germany, France, Italy, Belgium; the middle-ranked-anxiety group were from Denmark, Switzerland, Norway, Finland; the low-anxiety group were from Sweden, the Netherlands, the UK, Ireland. These groups do match the racial sub-classifications of these regions, as set out by C. S. Coon.[5]

Evidence suggests that in some areas, the hereditary contribution of ethnicity/race transcends host culture and climatic conditions. A study of suicides of foreigners in the USA (conducted in 1959), demonstrated that migrants committed suicide in largely proportion to the prevalence of suicide in their birth countries. American-Swedes committed suicide most often, followed by Austrians, Czechoslovaks, West Germans, with American-Mexicans committing suicide less often. Notably, immigrant suicides were double, treble or quadruple the rate of compatriots who remained in their homelands.[6]

Two separate studies were conducted in the USA on pain thresholds of racial groups. The first found: "Italians and Jews were described as tending to exaggerate this pain, while the Irish were depicted as stoical individuals who are able to take a great deal of pain."[7] A second, conducted by Tursky and Sternbach in 1965, studied American-born racial Irish, Italians, Jews and Yankees (WASP, Anglo-colonials). The highest to lowest pain thresholds were Irish, Yankee, Jewish, Italian. "[…] this would seem to make it not at all improbable that a genetic factor might underlie the different ethnic reactions to pain which Tursky and Sternbach have discovered."[8]

These few observations leave open the question of how many of these observable phenomena regarding immigrant groups can be traced to genetic differences and how many to persistent social conditioning within migrant cultures distinct from the majority host culture.[9] What we see is that there are grounds for thinking that aspects of character—however transmitted—can be inherited and shared among members of the same ethnicity or race.

ENDNOTES

1   Cyril Burt in Lynn, 1971, p. xii.

2   Lynn, 1971, p. 180.

3   Lynn, 1971, p. 93.

4   Lynn, 1971, p. 173.

5   Lynn, 1971, p. 161.

6   Lynn, 1971, p. 10.

7   Zborowski, 1952, quoted in Lynn, 1971, p. 169.

8   Lynn, 1971, p. 171.

9   See also the writings of Thomas Sowell on the ethnicity/race and associated culture carries over from home countries for immigrants.

# FASCIST RESPONSES
# TO ROMANTICISM

Igor Golomstock, historian of totalitarian art, claims, "the rational, scientific and ideological foundations of Communism, National Socialism and Fascism are not linked with any particular national culture, still less with a particular racial consciousness."[1] Some consider the propensity for totalitarianism as a racial characteristic.[2] Evidence for Golomstock's case comes from the differing policies towards the arts south of the Alps. Fascism in Italy took a different course to German National Socialism.

> This is the answer of Fascism: by means of the organization of people into groups in accordance with their useful activities, groups which will be grateful to their leaders—the captains of tens, hundreds and thousands of men—as they construct something similar to the pyramids, whose base is formed by the masses and whose apex is the State. No groups outside the State, no groups against the State, all groups within the State. The organization of practitioners of the free arts and professions into registered professional unions is the most specific and outstanding achievement of the Fascist regime.[3]

Fascism was nationalist but not essentially race-based.[4] Fascism assumed that the needs of the state and nation correlated to the needs of Italians, as a people and ethnicity. Mario Sironi (1885–1961) was a Futurist in the 1910s. Futurism was an assertively Modernist ideology in art that adulated the mechanical, new, utilitarian and mass produced, with a pronounced hostility towards national sentiment in conventional art,[5] while being nationalistic and chauvinist on an ethnic level. The Futurist creed has been cast as "their hatred of bourgeois culture, their cult of youth, strength and optimism, their love of danger, their belief in the future and contempt towards both past and present".[6] They set themselves against conventional artistic nationalism, instead taking sport, manufacturing, technology, and warfare as ideal forms of national advancement, not least because they were viewed as non-aesthetic. It is notable that Futurists who survived World War I became converts to Neo-classicism and/or Fascist nationalism, abandoning their machine aesthetic but retaining some radical utopianism. Sironi's work from around 1920 is a fusion of Metaphysical art and social realism, which has aspects of social commentary.

Sironi published a statement on Fascist art in "Manifesto of Mural Painting" in 1933.[7]

> Fascism is a style of life: it is life itself for Italians. No formula will ever succeed in completely expressing it, let alone defining it. Similarly, no formula will ever succeed in expressing, let alone defining, what is understood as Fascist art, that is to say, an art which is the plastic expression of the Fascist spirit. [...] *In the Fascist state art acquires a social function:* an educative function. It must translate the ethic of our times.[8]

This echoes Plato's conception of the arts as utilitarian and set to the goal of educating the aristocrat philosopher-guardians who should rule.

> *The individualist conception of 'art for art's sake' is dead.* As a result of this there is a deep incompatibility between the goals that Fascist art assigns itself and all the forms are born of the arbitrary, of individualization, of the particular aesthetic of a group, of a coterie, an academy.[9]

As a result, Sironi recommends mural painting as ideal activity for artists as it is communally achieved public work for the benefit of the nation.[10]

The outcome of serving ethnos and polis is achieved by setting aside notions of genius and individual taste. While Nazis expected artists to blunt their individual proclivities when they conflicted with the good of the ethnos—or for the artist's personal qualities to align with the good of the state, through a natural expression of their ethno-racial genius—the Italians recommended submission of individual to collective:

> A moral question arises for every artist. The artist must renounce this egocentricity which from now on can only sterilize his spirit, and become a 'militant' artist who serves

a moral ideal, subordinating his own individuality to collective work.[11]

For the Fascists, it is only by setting aside the Romantic ideal of the artist communing with himself and nature in the search for insight and transcendence that the artist can do the work of serving the ethnos and polis. There is no necessity to quote Soviet officials and creators on the even more communal and utilitarian purposes of art in the Communist state, one explicitly internationalist (in contrast to Fascist nationalism). This aspect of Fascism shows that Romanticism was viewed as (potentially) individualistically subversive, in communal terms, and antithetical to the good of the state, as guardian of the nation's welfare. It should also be noted that Fascism allowed a greater range of artistic styles than the Nazis did, so this distinction is neither strong nor complete. The style which received most official support from Fascists was Novecento, a blend of Romanticism, Early Renaissance and Metaphysical Art.[12] Novecento was supported by Margherita Sarfatti, the most prominent art critic in Italy and mistress of Mussolini, who opened Novecento exhibitions.[13] Metaphysical artists Carlo Carrà, Giorgio de Chirico and Giorgio Morandi joined or exhibited alongside Novecento and found Fascism compatible with their Romantic nationalism.

When the ethnos as ethnos is to be served, Romanticism can be supported or actively advanced by the governing nationalistic elite; when the state is to be served, Romanticism may not be seen as suitable and may be considered actually deleterious to the well-being of the state, due to its emphasis on individualism.

# ENDNOTES

1    Golomstock, 1990, p. 156.

2    Golomstock, 1990, p. 157.

3    M. Missoroli, O. Agresti, 1938, quoted in Golomstock, 1990, p. 117.

4    On the racial foundations for Fascist art, consider Carlo Carrà. "[…] Carrà asserted that Italians were the "race of great constructors" whose indigenous sense of geometry was responsible for the whole of Western European art." Emily Braun, "Mario Sironi's *Urban Landscapes*", in Matthew Affron, Mark Antliff (*eds.*), *Fascist Visions: Art and Ideology in France and Italy*, Princeton University Press, Princeton, 1997, p. 119.

5    "Destroy the cult of the past, the obsession with the ancients, pedantry and academic formalism. […] The dead shall be buried in the earth's deepest bowels!" Umberto Boccioni, et al. "Manifesto of the Futurist Painters" (1910), in Alex Danchev (*ed.*), *100 Artists' Manifestos: From the Futurists to the Stuckists*, Penguin, London, 2011, pp. 12–3.

6    Golomstock, 1990, p. 114.

7    It was also signed by (former Cubo-Futurist) Achille Funi, (former Futurist) Massimo Campligli and (former Metaphysical artist) Carlo Carrà.

8    Mario Sironi, "Manifesto of Mural Painting", 1933, in Harrison, 2003, pp. 424–6. See also Emily Braun, "Mario Sironi's Urban Landscapes", in Matthew Affron, Mark Antliff (*eds.*), *Fascist Visions: Art and Ideology in France and Italy*, Princeton University Press, Princeton, 1997.

9    *Ibid.*

10    For Sironi and Funi as leaders of Novecento and recipients of official Fascist commissions, see Golomstock, 1990, pp. 47–8.

11    *Ibid.*

12    See Flavia Frigeri, Janet Abramovicz, *Morandi, Balla, de Chirico and Italian Painting 1920–1950*, Tornabuoni Art, 2020. My review is at https://alexanderadamsart.wordpress.com/2020/08/23/italian-novecento-painting/.

13    Golomstock, 1990, pp. 40 and 55.

# DEBRIS,
# SEEN IN EPOCHAL TIME

Anselm Kiefer (b. 1945) was born in Germany in the final weeks of World War II, and his childhood, surrounded by the ruins of his hometown of Donaueschingen left a strong impression on him. Kiefer lived with images of burned buildings, crashed military aeroplanes, and destroyed machinery. In those years, survivors scavenged steel for a pittance. At this time, German street photographer Friedrich Seidenstücker (1882–1966) photographed Berlin's Tiergarten park shorn of vegetation, ground pummelled by military vehicles, and the *Trümmerfrauen* (German: rubble women), who formed chains to collect usable bricks from heaps of masonry. When Kiefer was freed of financial constraints, he moved to France and bought a former brick factory in Barjac, Gard, which he used as his studio. In that building, he made large installations out of rubble, cast concrete, earth, salvaged materials, sheet lead, straw, dried sunflowers, and other non-art materials. He recreated the Germany of his childhood, thinking of how rubble (over time) becomes soil in which plants and crops can grow. As an artist-alchemist, he turns debris into art.

Kiefer associates wartime debris with the Romantic aspirations of the Nazis. Kiefer detected in Hitler—as did Munch and Dalí[1]—an innate masochism and desire for failure, one of a specifically German character. The German nationalist worldview is epitomised by the lone traveller (as found in the landscape paintings of Friedrich) who dwells upon the past as he contemplates ruins in the wilderness. The ruin becomes a symbol of man's hubris, the cyclical decline of civilisations and the unassuageable power of nature. An embodiment of that Romantic melancholic yearning for a ruined landscape is to be found in the *Ruinenwert* (German: ruin value). This was an idea refined and popularised by German architect Albert Speer (1905–1981), chief architect of Nazi rule after the death Troost. Speer consulted with Hitler on the design of new civic buildings that would appear noble and grand when ruined. Speer wrote,

> By using special materials and by applying certain principles of statics, we should be able to build structures which even in a state of decay, after hundreds or (such were our reckonings) thousands of years would more or less resemble Roman models.[2]

If the nobility of the ancients was apparent in ruins of their buildings encountered today, so nobility might be accrued by the modern architect through the creation of buildings that would look magnificent as future ruins.

As already mentioned, in the ruin we find the fusion of man's handiwork and nature's action—taken by the Romantics as a refutation of Apollonian rationalism through the destructive power of Dionysian nature. The ruin, the picturesque, the grotto and the overgrown cemetery—and the cemetery isle—had resonance for Romantics beyond cognitive appreciation; such places spoke to the immortal soul and the aesthetic feeling within man, which distinguished him from the beast. The ruin was a fragment, and fragmentary qualities were lauded in Romantic aesthetics, who wrote in fragmentary aphorisms.[3] Kiefer painted the Speer-designed Berliner Neuen Reichkanzlei in ruins, accelerated from new to ruined in one decade; at the centre of the space he placed a palette and dedicated the picture as a monument to the unknown painter. It was an ironical tribute to the lost artists of history and the "failed" Austrian painter who founded a thousand-year Reich that lasted a dozen years. Troost's *Ehrentempel* (German: honour temple) in Munich, erected in 1935 to commemorate Hitler's failed *putsch* of 1923, was also painted by Kiefer. The ruins of the Reich were seen by Kiefer in terms of cyclical civilisational decline, a tragedy of history. Kiefer was also aware of Heidegger's statements about the temple on the land being of the people, and he saw Heidegger's observations on art as tied to the tragedy of Germany and the Reich's ruined temples to the *Alte Kämpfer* (German: old fighters).

In Kiefer's paintings—deliberately subjected to oxidisation, fading and cracking, executed partially in industrial and non-art materials—the debris of history is a matter of deep time, geological time, which surpasses the lifetime of a man. His interests stretch back to the civilisations of Egypt and Mesopotamia. He sees layers of history forming above the past, concealing but not erasing. He is the artist as archaeol-ogist. Soil becomes a palimpsest, where civilisations write their stories across the land but only impermanently and subject to alteration and dilution. Kiefer's art presents putative parallels between events and phenomena apparently distant, tying the far past with recent events, seeing recurring patterns and persistent symbols.

The absence of unequivocal condemnation of Nazi history in his art led to criticism of Kiefer early in his career.[4] In the 1970s, Kiefer paint-ed interiors of wooden buildings, referencing mystic Mechthild von Magdeburg and Friedrich. Friedrich's ghost seems to linger in Kiefer's photographs of German landscapes made in the mid-1970s, where the faded printing resembles the mists of the Romantic sublime. Growing up in the Black Forest region, Kiefer absorbed tales of the heroic past and Nordic myths associated with the wildest region of Germany, min-gling references in a non-narrative manner. One of his earliest mature works was a large book composed of a series of woodcuts of German military heroes. A large wall-painting version was made by the artist pasting the roughly printed pages on to a canvas, that was subsequently overpainted. Kiefer gave this work—and the book—the title *Teutoburg-er Wald* (*Teutoburg Forest*) (1977), after the site of the victory of the German tribes over Varus's legions. In *Varus* (1976) Kiefer depicts the interior of a forest, inscribed with names of famous Germans, including von Kleist, Fichte, Field Marshal von Schlieffen and Hermann, bane of Varus. The ambiguity of Kiefer's national, mythological, and Romantic subjects left liberal Germans and international art critics suspicious of his views regarding National Socialism.[5] Any evocations of ancestors, national myths and the ties of blood and soil conjured through paint inevitably confront us with a resilient persistent network of truths, fic-tions, and powerful emotions, which we must dare to study honestly and speak of frankly.

# ENDNOTES

1    Attributed to Dalí by Robert Descharnes: "Furthermore, I saw Hitler as a masochist obsessed with the *idée fixe* of starting a war and losing it in heroic style. In a word, he was preparing for one of those *actes gratuits* which were then highly approved of by our group. My persistence in seeing the mystique of Hitler from a Surrealist point of view and my obstinacy in trying to endow the sadistic element in Surrealism with a religious meaning (both exacerbated by my method of paranoiac-critical analysis, which threatened to destroy automatism and its inherent narcissism) led to a number of wrangles and occasional rows with [André] Breton and his friends."

2    Speer, quoted in Golomstock, 1990, p. 281.

3    "Many of the works of the ancients have become fragments. Many modern works are fragments as soon as they are written. [...] A dialogue is a chain or garland of fragments. [...] A fragment, like a miniature work of art, has to be entirely isolated from the surrounding world and be complete in itself like a porcupine." Friedrich Schlegel, "Athenaeum Fragments", 1798–1800, in Harrison, 2000, pp. 904–6.

4    Biro, 2013, p. 10.

5    "The political and artistic leaders he depicted were all figures the Nazis used to support their cause. Hence the canvas [*Ways of Worldly Wisdom—Hermann's Battle* (1978–80)] suggested that culture helps to constitute national identity, implying that artists make a form of politics, both willingly and unwillingly. Furthermore, the representation was both critical and seductive." Biro, 2013, p. 24. Arthur Danto accused Kiefer of flirting with Nazism. See Schama, 2004, p. 133 and footnote 109, p. 588.

# LETTER[1]

Berlin, 20 October 2006

Dear Sue

I knew Berlin primarily through two photographers: Heinrich Zille[2] and Friedrich Seidenstücker. In Zille's photographs of sculptors' studios of the immediate post-Bismarck era (1890–1900) one can see the statues being made for Tiergarten. In Seidenstücker's photographs of 1945–50 one sees those same sculptures maimed, felled corralled into barbed-wire enclosures.

And yet here Zille is known best as a draughtsman of sentimental vignettes. Everywhere one sees his drawings reproduced. I came across a Zille Hof[3]—a collection of junk stalls under railway arches.

In the Alte Nationalgalerie there are two paintings by Hummel[4] of a huge granite dish being cut and polished and another of it set in the Lustgarten, both making great play of its glassy surface which he captures so well. Indeed, it seems to exhaust him. In the Lustgarten painting he seems to have nothing left for the surroundings—they don't convince or they don't hold us. And afterwards one can walk from the museum to the Lustgarten and see that same bowl pitted with bullet holes.

Böcklin is a much greater painter than I had realised. One just can't see him in Britain. *Die Toteninsel* cannot be reproduced. It has great variety of shade, surprising oranges and violets. It can't be appreciated on the page. He is a serious artist and I can see now why he is held in high esteem in Germany—why de Chirico fell under his influence.

JCC Dahl was represented by a couple of cloud studies. Of course, he was a Dresden artist but I knew him from Bergen (and Oslo).[5]

Die Alte Nationalgalerie is beautifully restored and a better building than our National Gallery. I won't draw up a balance sheet of pluses and minuses on the various collections nor even of the Berlin experience as a whole. One only understands in retrospect what one takes from an experience.

In Hamburger Bahnhof[6] I found one quote which I will give you in its entirety.

> *Trümmer sind am sich Zukunft. Weil alles, was ist, vergeht. Es gibt dieses wunderbare Kapitel bei Jesaja, in dem is heisst: Uber euren Stadten wird Gras waschsen. Dieser Spruch hat mich immer fasziniert, schon als Kind. Diese Poesie, die Tatsache, dass man beides zugleich sieht. Jesaja sieht die Stadt und die anderen Schichten daruber, das Gras und wieder eine Stadt, das Gras und wieder eine Stadt.*

Kiefer, 2005

["Rubble is the future. Because everything that is, passes. There is a wonderful chapter in Isaiah that says: grass will grow over your cities. This sentence has always fascinated me, even as a child. This poetry is the fact that you see both things at the same time. Isaiah sees the city and the different layers over it, the grass, and then another city, the grass and then another city again."]

Evidence enough of that here in Berlin—the vacant lots and grassy mounds are everywhere to be seen, like Zille's sandy scrubland traversed by barefoot children or Seidenstücker's tank-trampled Tiergarten.

Vi ses,[7]

aja

# ENDNOTES

1    Letter written by the author to Sue Prideaux, author of *Edvard Munch: Behind the Scream*, Yale University Press, London, 2005, on his first visit to Berlin, his future home from 2007 to 2014. First published in *Alexander Adams: Ruins and Landscapes/Ruinen und Landschaften*, Golconda Fine Art Books, 2007.

2    Heinrich Zille (1858–1929), Berlin-based German photographer and graphic artist.

3    German: courtyard.

4    Johann Erdmann Hummel (1769–1852), German landscape painter, painter of *The Granite Dish of Berlin Lustgarten* (1831) and a second painting showing the making of the dish, both paintings in the Alte Nationalgalerie, Berlin.

5    A visit by the author to Norway in 2001.

6    A former train station in Berlin, converted into a contemporary art museum, including in the permanent collection art by Kiefer.

7    Norwegian: see you.

# APPENDIX:
# THE ARTWORK OF
# ALEXANDER ADAMS

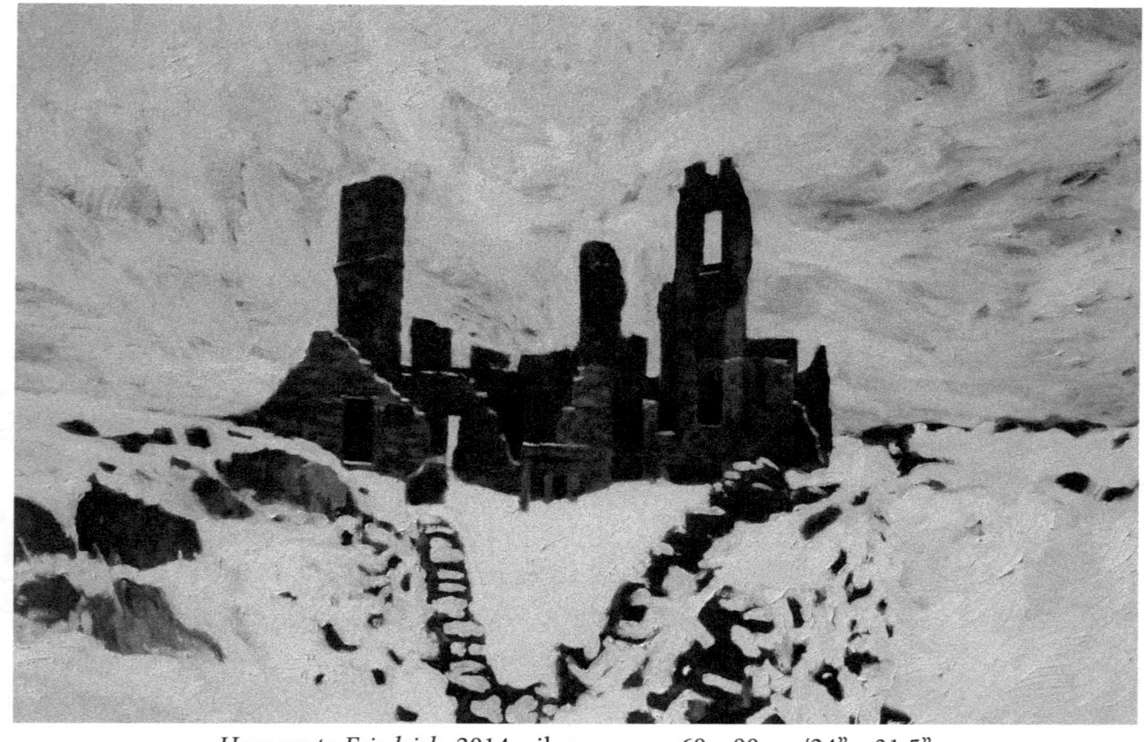

*Homage to Friedrich,* 2014, oil on canvas, 60 x 80 cm/24" x 31.5"

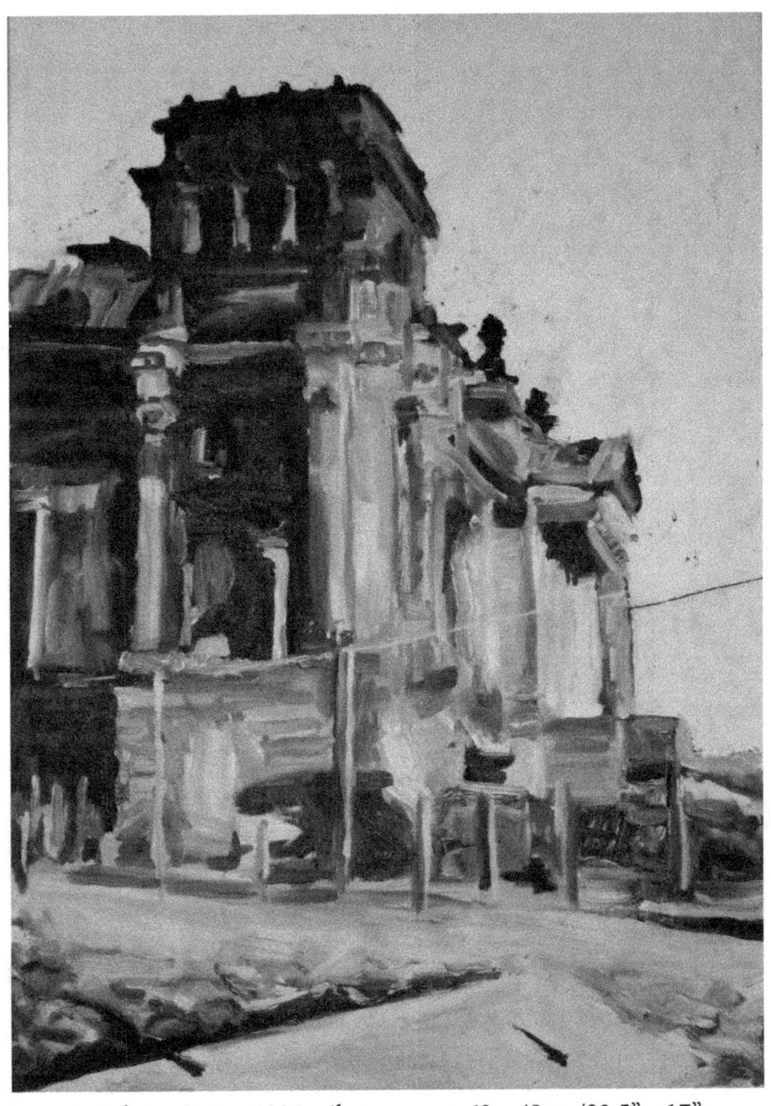

*Reichstag Ruins,* 1995, oil on canvas, 60 x 43cm/23.5" x 17"

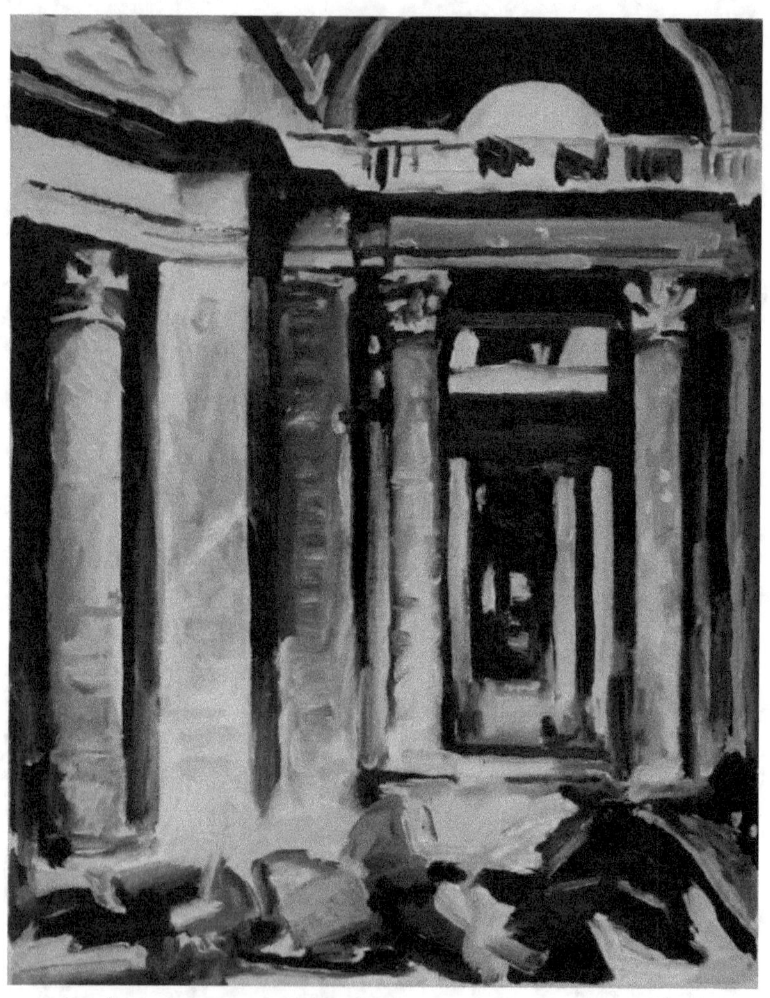

*Reichstag Interior,* c. 2014, oil on canvas, 24 x 18 cm/9.5" x 7"

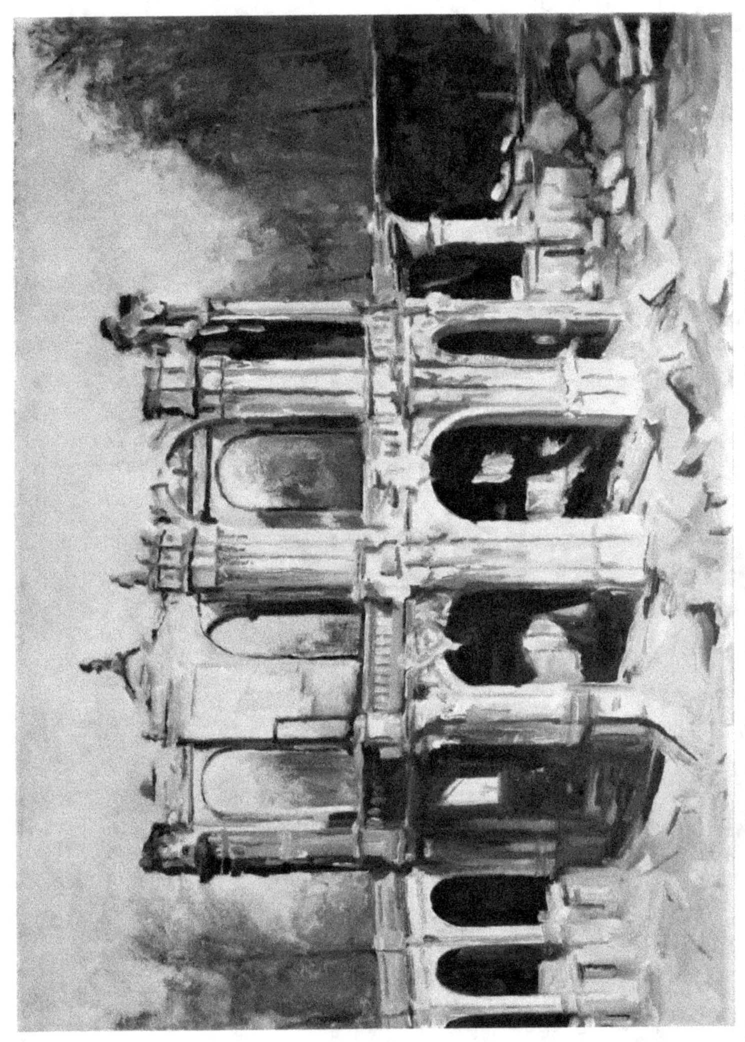

*Dresden Ruins*, 2011, oil on canvas, 30 x 40 cm/12" x 16"

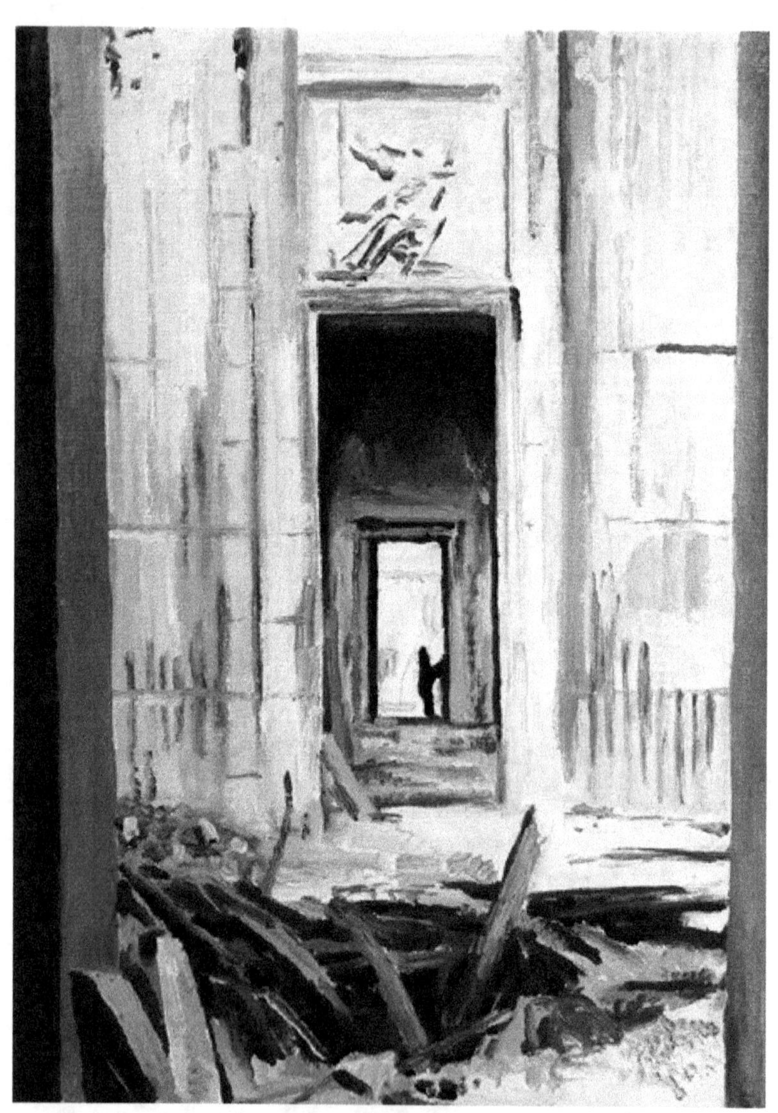

*Neue Reichskanzlei*, c. 2014, oil on canvas, 24 x 18 cm/9.5" x 7"

# BIBLIOGRAPHY


Peter Adams, *The Arts of the Third* Reich, Thames & Hudson, London, 1992

Matthew Biro, *Anselm Kiefer*, Phaidon, London, 2013

M.C. Bradbrook, *Ibsen, The Norwegian: A Revaluation*, Chatto & Windus, 1966

Bryson Burroughs, "The Isle of the Dead by Arnold Böcklin", *Bulletin of the Metropolitan Museum of Art*, Vol. 21, No. 6, pp. 146-8, New York, June 1926

Jean Clay, *Romanticism*, Phaidon, London, 1981

Joan L. Clinefelter, *Artists for the Reich: Culture and Race from Weimar to Nazi Germany*, Berg, Oxford, 2005

Lilian R. Furst, *Romanticism in Perspective*, MacMillan, London, 1969

Joseph Arthur de Gobineau, H. Holtz (*commentary*), *The Moral and Intellectual Diversity of Races, with Particular Reference to their Respective Influence in the Civil and Political History of Mankind*, 1853-5, J.B. Lippincott, Philadelphia, 1856

Igor Golomstock, *Totalitarian Art*, Harper Collins, London, 1990

Lionel Gossman, "Jugendstil in Firestone: The Jewish Illustrator E.M. Lilien (1874-1925)", *The Princeton University Library Chronicle*, Vol. 66, No. 1, pp. 11-78, Princeton, Autumn 2004

Charles Harrison, Paul Wood, Jason Gaiger (*eds.*), *Art in Theory: 1815-1900*, Blackwell, Oxford, 1998

Charles Harrison, Paul Wood, Jason Gaiger (*eds.*), *Art in Theory: 1648-1815*, Blackwell, Oxford, 2000

Charles Harrison, Paul Wood (*eds.*), *Art in Theory: 1900-2000*, Blackwell, Oxford, second edition 2003

Martin Heidegger, David Farrell Krell (*ed., trans.*), *Basic Writings*, Harper, London, 2008

Martin Heidegger, David Farrell Krell (*ed., trans.*), *Nietzsche: Volume I*, 1961, Routledge & Kegan, London, 1981

Joseph Leo Koerner, *Caspar David Friedrich and the Subject of Landscape*, Reaktion Books, London, second edition 2009

Ingar Sletten Kolloen, Deborah Dawkin (*trans.*), Erik Skuggevik (*trans.*), *Knut Hamsun: Dreamer and Dissenter*, Yale University Press, New Haven, 2009

Jon Røyne Kyllingstad, *Measuring the Master Race: Physical Anthropology in Norway, 1890-1945*, Cambridge University Press, 2014

Cesare Lombroso, *The Man of Genius*, 1888, Walter Scott, London, 1917

Richard Lynn, *Personality and National Character*, Pergamon Press, Oxford, 1971

Max Nordau, *Degeneration*, 1892-3, William Heineman, London, 1898

Olaf Peters (*ed.*), *Degenerate Art: The Attack on Modern Art in Nazi Germany 1937*, Prestel/Neue Galerie, Munich/New York, 2014

Sue Prideaux, *Edvard Munch: Behind the Scream*, Yale University Press, London, 2005

Alfred Rosenberg, *The Myth of the Twentieth Century*, 1930, third edition 1937, undated translation, https://archive.org/details/alfredrosenbergmythofthetwentiethcentury/

Simon Schama, *Landscape and Memory*, 1995, Harper Perennial, London, 2004

Peter Sjølyst-Jackson, *Troubling Legacies: Migration, Modernism, and Fascism in the Case of Knut Hamsun*, Continuum, London, 2010

Staatliche Kunstammlungen Dresden (*ed.*), *Dreams of Freedom: Ro-*

*manticism in Russia and Germany*, Hirmer Verlag, Munich, 2022

Madame de Staël, Morroe Berger (*ed., trans.*), *Madame de Staël on Politics, Literature and National Character*, Sidgwick & Jackson, London, 1964

Jakob Stougaard-Nielsen, "Nordic Nature: From Romantic Nationalism to the Anthropocene", in *Introduction to Nordic Cultures*, pp. 165-180, University College London Press, London, 2020

Despina Stratigakos, *Hitler's Northern Utopia*, 2020, Princeton University Press, Princeton, 2022

Lynne M. Swarts, *Gender, Orientalism and the Jewish Nation: Women in the Work of Ephraim Moses Lilien at the German* Fin de Siècle, Bloomsbury Visual Arts, London, 2020

Guy Tourlamain, "*Völkisch*" *Writers and National Socialism: A Study of Right-Wing Political Culture in Germany, 1890-1960*, Peter Lang AG, Bern, 2014

William Vaughan, *Friedrich*, Phaidon, London, 2004

H.G. Wells, *Anticipations of the Reaction of Mechanical and Scientific Progress upon Human Life and Thought*, 1901, Chapman & Hall, London, eighth edition 1902

Josef Wiehr, *Knut Hamsun, his personality and his outlook upon life*, Smith College, Northampton, Massachusetts, 1922

Johann Joachim Winckelmann, Henry Fuseli (*trans.*), *Reflections on the Painting and Sculpture of the Greeks*, Fuseli, London, 1765

Barnaby Wright (*ed.*), *Edvard Munch: Masterpieces from Bergen*, Paul Holberton, London, 2022

# INDEX

www.ingramcontent.com/pod-product-compliance
Lightning Source LLC
LaVergne TN
LVHW020044160726
843469LV00043B/1511